22 May 96.
Anosho .

BERLIN

FACADES: POUR 44

Jules Laforgue

the whole length of Unter den Linden as far as the Imperial Palace, on which the flag announcing the Emperor's residence in Berlin will already be unfurled.

Entry into the Prussian capital by rail is cold and dreary. It is not like arriving in Paris after having passed gay country houses and gardens, typical Parisian suburbs, followed by those districts with tall buildings covered with posters, billboards and flowering balconies, all swarming with people and shops, on both sides of the noisy operations of the station. Here the country consists of nothing but sand, with dark pine trees on both sides of the track; and then one comes suddenly on the highways leading into the city, and low houses daubed with that potato or macadam color so characteristic of the local scene. No billboards, balconies, or shutters break the monotony. On the street level there are steps leading down into shops. One must see these houses to understand how sinister a façade without balconies and especially without shutters (which gives the windows the appearance of mere holes) can be; and to appreciate the real beauty of the façade of an ordinary house in Paris.

It is twilight, a late August twilight. In the

BERLIN
The City and the Court

BY

JULES LAFORGUE

Translated and with an
Introduction by
WILLIAM JAY SMITH

Photographs by Simone Sassen

TURTLE POINT PRESS

NEW YORK

Design: Christine Taylor
Composition: Wilsted & Taylor Publishing Services

ISBN 1-885983-02-6
Library of Congress Number 95-061968

ACKNOWLEDGMENTS

The preparation of this volume was made possible, in part, by a grant from the Program for Translations of the National Endowment for the Humanities, an independent Federal agency.

The translator is also grateful to the Camargo Foundation, Cassis, France, where, thanks to a residency in 1986, the translation was completed.

Several chapters, in slightly different form, appeared in *The Yale Review* and in *Selected Writings of Jules Laforgue*, edited and translated by William Jay Smith, Grove Press. Chapter 2 appeared in part in *Talisman: A Journal of Contemporary Poetry and Poetics*. Parts of the introduction, in slightly different form, appeared in the *International Herald Tribune* and *The New Criterion*. The translator wishes to thank the editors of these books and journals for permission to reprint.

With permission of Simon & Schuster and Laurence Pollinger Ltd., several paragraphs in my text are reprinted from *The Kaisers* by Theo Aronson, copyright 1971 by Theo Aronson, an original Bobbs-Merrill publication.

For assistance on both my visits to Berlin in 1986 and 1995 I am extremely grateful to Dr. Sabine Bohle and to Professor and Mrs. Harald Preuss. On my first visit I received additional assistance from John K. Menzies, Cultural Attaché at the American Embassy, Wolfgang Brandt, Program Assistant, Amerika Haus, West Berlin, and Thomas G. Blake, Command Information Specialist of the Public Affairs Office of the Headquarters of the United States Command and the United States Army in Berlin. For help on my 1995 visit, I am grateful to Owen Levy and Peter M. Dollé.

My greatest debt is to David Arkell, the author of *Looking for Laforgue: An Informal Biog-*

raphy; without his careful reading of my early draft and his corrections and additions to it, this final text would not have been possible. I am also grateful to M. Jean-Louis Debauve for additional information and to my wife, Sonja Haussmann Smith, for constant attention and encouragement. Much of the phrasing in this final version is hers. For any errors that remain I am solely responsible.

W. J. S.

CONTENTS

BERLIN

INTRODUCTION

Poets are proverbially poor and usually consigned to garrets but the French poet Jules Laforgue (1860–87) was the exception. He was not rich, but he lived like a prince in a royal palace and there produced in his short life work that left its mark on the literature of his own country and an even greater mark on later generations of writers in England and America. Through the intervention of his friends, the writer Paul Bourget and the art collector and critic Charles Ephrussi (who may have served as one of the models for Proust's Charles Swann), Laforgue went in 1881 to Berlin as French reader to the Empress Augusta. The Empress, a descendant of Catherine the Great of Russia, having grown up in Goethe's Weimar, despised most things German and spoke only French. It was Laforgue's duty to read to her twice a day from French books and newspapers. He occupied a large, high-ceilinged, elaborately furnished apartment, with olive-green walls, ebony woodwork, and dark wall hangings, on the ground floor of the Palace of the Princesses on Unter den Linden, where he had fires in every room and was looked after by his own servant. "Opposite me is the Royal Guard House," he wrote to a friend, "all military bands and pointing cannon. On my left, the Opera and the Palace. On my right, a mass of columns and statues. I have five windows looking out in all directions. I can see nothing but monuments. And officers with pale monocles." He resigned his position and left Berlin in the winter of 1886 to travel to London, where he married Leah Lee, a young woman with whom he had studied English. The couple returned to Paris, where Laforgue died of tuberculosis on August 20, 1887, four days after his twenty-seventh birthday.

Laforgue's palace routine was indeed boring and boredom became one of his favorite subjects, but it allowed him to produce two volumes of poetry, with a third ready for publication at the time of his death. In his last and greatest poems, published posthumously, he was the first to make effective use of *vers libre*. An exhibition of Impressionist paintings in Berlin at the Gurlitt Gallery prompted Laforgue to write the first, and still the best, essay on Impressionism. Laforgue was a master of irony, and it is, of course, supremely ironic that, while quartered in a palace, he should be the first poet to introduce into poetry all the sordid details of modern life. It was this aspect of Laforgue that T. S. Eliot took over, sometimes literally, in his early work, and that has influenced much of poetry since. Laforgue's book of tales (*Moralités légendaires*), with its blend of parody and high seriousness, served as a point of departure for James Joyce and subsequently for many other writers and dramatists. During his five-year sojourn, Laforgue was constantly taking notes on court life and on the city. He incorporated many of these into his poems and stories; others he kept for the book on Berlin that he had planned for some time. That book, *Berlin, la cour et la ville*, not published until 1922, is still little known even in France.

Laforgue has been called the French Keats, and like Keats, in his poems and letters, he made full use of his senses. Writing of Berlin as well, he brings forcefully to bear all his sensory perceptions. Many people have written about imperial Berlin but no one has told us better than Laforgue exactly what it was like to be there. He not only sees the military presence in his brilliant description of the goings-on at the Royal Guard House below his windows but he also hears that presence in the clicking of spurs in the palace hallways and the scraping of a saber along the pavement.

He tells us how everything looked at the Opera Ball but also how it smelled—of a mixture of *eau de cologne* and the floor wax that had been very generously applied. He shows us exactly what Unter den Linden was like at every hour of the day and night: he tells of the poverty of the morning hours with young women in their cheap hats, the loads of red cabbage going by, the milk carts with their teams of muzzled dogs; he records the flashing change of the guard at noon and the bright bourgeois activity of the afternoon, followed by the still evening when the avenue became a hallway for the glittering officers moving toward the Royal Palace for the court balls. He paints a startling picture of night on Friedrichstrasse with bloated Prince George in his general's uniform strolling along in pursuit of his pleasures with his high-sprung, finely balanced carriage following behind him; with the prostitutes bending over the gutter to eat their hot sausages. He shows us close-up the shop windows, the music halls, the beer gardens. He reports what people wore, what they ate, what they smoked. He gives us the very texture of life, and no detail is too insignificant to escape his attention. On the crushed top hat of an old coachman he sees attached a "new patent leather cockade that caught the sunlight like a black diamond." And he glimpses, in passing, the polychrome china parrots on the palm branches in the Empress's little conservatory. The effect of the whole is that of one of those Impressionist paintings Laforgue admired, where all the bright individual brush strokes add up to a scene that is singularly alive and moving.

In his tales Laforgue made imaginative use of the material that he presents here in straightforward terms. In "Salomé," in particular, we recognize the presence of the German court. "Salomé" is a parody of Flaubert's "Hérodias," but while Flaubert found the sources of his tale in the library, Laforgue looked around him and put down what he saw. The Tetrarchic Palace, hewn out of black basalt, is the royal Schloss, that monumental structure that Laforgue describes exactly in *Berlin*. The Tetrarch Emerald-Archetypas is modeled on Emperor William I. Without his close view of the Prussian officers around him Laforgue could never have described the Princes of the North so precisely: "girded, pomaded, gloved, and uniformed, with full-flowing beards and parted hair (with locks curved down around their temples to give tone to the profiles stamped on their medallions) . . . waiting, one hand holding the helmet on the right hip while the other—with the prancing gesture of a stallion catching a whiff of gunpowder—fidgeted with the saber on the left one."

In 1871 the Prussian nobility composed less than one percent of the urban population but it wielded immense influence. The aristocracy completely dominated the guards stationed in Berlin and Potsdam; in the officer corps of one regiment alone there were thirteen princes and ten counts. The cavalry regiments boasted thirty-four princes and fifty-one counts. The military, thus closely linked to the court, was everywhere and its power pervaded every aspect of life. Half the population of Berlin, Laforgue observes, seemed to be in uniform, and the half that wasn't dressed as if it were. The city was living, he says, in a "slight state of siege."

In 1986, on a hot summer day like the one Laforgue had described a century before, I visited Berlin for the first time. The city, split down the middle by a wall that cut through every segment like a jagged bolt of lightning, was, it seemed to me, living under a full state of siege.

In Lichterfelde in the American sector of West Berlin, the Royal Central Cadet School, where Prussian officers had been trained, largely destroyed by bombs, was then occupied by U.S. forces as Andrews Barracks. The sentimental frieze in the Field Marshals' Hall there, which for Laforgue depicted the spirit of the German soldier proud to place "his huge hand on the Parisian volcano," was gone. The main stop of the tourist bus in East Berlin was the mammoth Soviet War Memorial in Treptow Park, where five thousand Soviet soldiers were buried, and where, in an adjacent beer garden, a band played, very much as it would have in Laforgue's time. The city that was striving at the turn of the century to be a world capital had in-

Unter den Linden, May 1989.

deed become one, the capital of a divided world that was all one armed camp.

On Unter den Linden, under ragged linden trees, a gift of the Hungarians set out in neat pathetic rows, a few earnest, ill-clad figures wandered as if on a dusty, rarely used stage set. Where the lively Café Bauer once stood at the corner of Unter den Linden and Friedrichstrasse the Linden Corso Restaurant served up mammoth portions of bad food in a dark cavernous interior. Nearby was a bookstore stocked with pristine mounds of unsold copies of Lenin's works and little else.

On the terrace outside the Palace of the Princesses, which had been restored as the Opera Café, a small group of beer-drinkers was seated under umbrellas. No one was inside when I entered what had been Laforgue's apartment. The café consisted of one large, low-ceilinged room with bright orange walls, tiny tables, and a grand piano in one corner. On the windowsills were pots of schefflera and mother-in-law's tongue.

Pushing aside the thin white curtains, I gazed across at the Royal Guard House (then, as now, called the New Guard House). Beyond a sea of parked cars, I watched a squad of East German guardsmen file from the neighboring Arsenal. With the familiar goose-step they made their way, propelled like mechanical dolls, toward the guard house, inside of which the East German authorities had lit an eternal flame to honor "the victims of fascism and militarism."

On the eve of V-E Day this year, I again visited Unter den Linden. The interior of the Palace of the Princesses has been completely remodeled and rechristened the Opera Palace. It contains four restaurants; Laforgue's apartment has been given a glitzier look, a long bar, and a raised platform in one corner on which a jazz combo holds forth. Below the windows the only signs of military activity were police cars lined up on both sides of the street in preparation for a demonstration by leftist students at Humboldt University next to the New Guard House. On the iron railing of the university was a poster showing a Soviet soldier smiling and holding cupped in his hands the decapitated head of a statue of Hitler. In the middle of the street was a large metal barge capped with grass and trees put there by the Greens, the words "The desert is in us" painted on its side. No guards stood outside the New Guard House, the interior design of which has been restored to what it was during the Weimar Republic. An enlarged bronze replica of a statue by Käthe Kollwitz, *Mother with Her Dead Son*, rests in the center and below it the words "To the victims of war and tyranny."

I found another vivid reminder of that tyranny opposite Humboldt University between the Opera and the Old Library at the center of Opera Square, which Laforgue used to pass each day on his way to read to the Empress. I saw several young Germans gathered in a circle, kneeling at times and all gazing intently below them. What they were looking at I had been looking for; I walked over to join them. There below us was the memorial to the bonfire of May 10, 1933, when thousands of Nazi sympathizers burned some twenty thousand books considered decadent or un-German. Entitled *Library*, the monument is the work of the Israeli sculptor Micha Ullman. It consists of an underground room lined with exactly enough stark white empty shelves to hold the number of books burned, among them works by German writers Thomas Mann, Bertolt Brecht, and Albert Einstein, as well as others by Ernest Hemingway, Jack London, and Marcel Proust. As I gazed down, a shaft of sunlight like a torch lit up one side of the empty library with a haunting effect. It accentuated a terrible emptiness akin to that of the unearthed white solitary cells below the Gestapo headquarters, where prisoners were kept and tortured. In the pavement beside the Old Library, two plaques explain the occasion of the memorial. On one are inscribed the words of the German poet Heinrich Heine, commenting on book-burning in 1820: "This is only a prelude. Where they burn books, in the end they will also burn people."

I returned to the square on V-E Day and found that rain had fallen as it had fifty years ago when Russian troops entered Berlin. It had clouded over the glass window so that *Library* below was just a blur but still several Germans struggled to make out the empty shelves. It was as if nature was obscuring for them what, even with the greatest vigilance, was difficult to face.

Since the day fifty years ago when Berliners came up from their cellars to examine the ruins of their city, they have been trying to fill in the empty spaces among the mounds of rubble, but much emptiness remains even after all the years of clearing, construction, and reconstruction. Berlin is the only city in the world the heart of

Demonstration, Lustgarten, East Berlin,
November 1989.

which is empty, and in a city harboring so many ghosts, it is perhaps natural that this emptiness, which extends physically and psychologically so far, will not be easy to fill. Potsdamer-Platz, the bustling center of imperial Berlin, from whose imposing station, the train, the second built in Germany, took the Emperor and the Empress regularly to the Babelsberg Palace in Potsdam, is now a great wasteland, the vacancy of which has been accentuated by the removal of the Wall. Before the government returns here finally between 1998 and 2000, this area is to be replaced by a huge business complex dominated by Daimler-Benz and Sony, which will make this its European headquarters. It is a bitter irony that the two allies defeated in World War II should today erect such a monumental display of economic world power in a wasteland adjacent to Hitler's Bunker. Nearby, below the remains of the Wertheim department store, the vacant underground stretches are being addressed in a different manner. The store's vaults have been turned into a disco called Tresor, where the young gather after midnight to dance to "techno" music while strobe lights play on metal grilles and empty deposit boxes.

The Palace of William I on Unter den Linden was, as Laforgue described it, of "that dull ocher found almost everywhere, and which to the new arrival seems the dominant tone of the capital." Only the Emperor and the Empress, with four or five attendants, lived there, the Emperor on the ground floor, where from his famous corner window he stood at attention every day at noon when the guard filed by. Their private apartments were "filled to overflowing with an odd assortment of rather inelegant Christmas presents; the large number of marble vases and little modern tables and chairs is especially deplorable."

The building, with its overflowing Christmas presents, no longer exists, but it came to mind when I discovered that modern Berlin seems to be making a fetish of wrapping its empty buildings and offering them up as presents to itself. The first such wrapping occurred in 1993. East German authorities in 1950 had blown up what remained of the Royal Palace and replaced it in the mid-1970s with the Palace of the Republic, an ugly gigantic rectangle of what looks like burnt-sienna isinglass, now condemned because of the asbestos it contains. Catherine Feff, a French artist, painted on vinyl one hundred feet high and three hundred feet

wide a *trompe l'oeil* façade that was hung over the
Palace of the Republic on scaffolding donated
by the Thyssen steelworks; it reproduced exactly
the four-story ocher façade with the windows
and balustrades of the original design of the
seventeenth-century architect Andreas Schlüter.
For several months thousands of people flocked
behind the façade to a special exhibition entitled
"The Castle?" Several businessmen sponsoring
the project put forward a proposal that would
cost a billion marks (about six hundred million
dollars) to tear down the Palace of the Republic
and replace it by at least the exterior of the old
Schloss. They wanted to make a gift of this exterior to the government; the government would
then be free to build whatever it found appropriate inside. It is significant that the title of the
exhibition was followed by a question mark:
when the *trompe-l'oeil* wrapping came down, no
decision had been taken regarding the castle.
And apparently the question mark still holds,
for the glaring Communist brown-glass box remains, dominant as ever, empty and unusable.

Berlin gave itself an even greater present with
what was called *Wrapped Reichstag, Project for
Berlin.* At the Radisson Plaza, the old Commu-

nist Palast Hotel overlooking the Spree where I stayed, the wording was slightly different. Anticipating a huge tourist turnout for the June event, an announcement in my room called attention to "the ultimate cultural event in 1995: The German Reichstag wrapped up by Christo." That "wrapping-up," which the German Bundestag had voted 292 to 228 to allow Christo to undertake, has been described in endless detail in the international press from what Christo and his collaborator, or as she now insists on being called, his co-artist wife, Jeanne-Claude, term their "software period," when Christo did all the sketches, maquettes, and engravings that were put on sale on the Kurfürstendamm to finance the project until the "hardware period" when the wrapping, with a million square feet of silver polypropylene fabric and nine miles of blue rope, was finally carried out. What has not been told about the project, which became a boon to the economy of East Germany, where entire towns were employed in the manufacture of the fabric, the thread, and the rope, is how it came about. The story making the rounds of Berlin when I was there, although apocryphal perhaps, may bear repeating. In 1971 Mike Cullen, an American long resident in Berlin, sent Christo a postcard of the Reichstag, suggesting that he come to wrap it. Christo replied indignantly that he was not interested and that he did not take suggestions; he alone decided what to wrap. When it was brought to his attention that Georgi Dimitrov (1882–1949), the co-founder of the Bulgarian Communist party and later president of the Bulgarian People's Republic, had been falsely accused of setting the Reichstag fire, Christo, himself a Bulgarian, changed his mind and decided to offer the wrapped Reichstag to Berlin and to the world, as well as to the memory of his compatriot. Also perhaps as a sixtieth-birthday present to himself and his wife.

Before the Reichstag wrapping could begin, a final obstacle had to be dealt with: the nest of a falcon was discovered above the building's main entrance. The Bird Protection Association, called in for consultation, finally reluctantly allowed the nest to be moved to the roof of the Palace of the President across the way.

It was perhaps fitting that a falcon should find itself at the center of such a monumental undertaking because that other bird of prey, the eagle, was the omnipresent emblem of Prussian power. Karl Friedrich Schinkel (1781–1841), the architect who designed so much of Neo-classical Berlin, including the Altes Museum and the New Guard House, also designed a peaked Prussian military helmet (commonly known as the Pickelaube) that featured the resplendent Prussian eagle. Although Schinkel modeled the Altes Museum on the Roman Pantheon, he never lost interest in medieval architecture. The Babelsberg Palace, which he began in 1835 and which was completed ten years later by Johann Heinrich Strack (1805–80), is pure Neo-Gothic. Modeled on Windsor Castle, which the Empress Augusta admired on a visit to England, it has more than "a flash of that hysteria" which, Christopher Isherwood in *Goodbye to Berlin* tells us, "flickers always behind every grave, gray Prussian façade." In one of its small rooms, perpendicular fan vaults duplicate the quiet lacelike beauty of St. George's Chapel, Windsor Castle, but just outside on the yellow Brandenburg brick a hideous sculpture depicts a particularly vicious eagle, its claws firmly clasping a doe that dangles down over the terrace. I went to visit the Palace, which Laforgue describes at the beginning of his book and which had been off limits at the time of my first visit; the Berlin Wall ran along below it and the windows of the pump house that it intersected had been boarded up to prevent escapes. The East Germans had covered over the Gothic walls of the interior in which they had installed a museum of local pre-history. Adjacent to the Schloss they had constructed an ugly square structure called an Academy for State and Law, a training school for the Secret Police. The Palace is now being restored to contain, as it once did, memorials of the various military campaigns of William I. Behind the palace is a monument commemorating the campaign of 1849, which earned for him the nickname of "grapeshot prince," with a sculpture by August Kiss (1802–65) depicting the archangel Michael slaying a dragon. In William's study and bedroom are displayed various desk ornaments, mementoes of his career as a cavalryman, an inkwell enclosed in a saddle topped with a riding cap, spurs hanging on the sides, a plaque with horseshoes at each corner, a bell resting on horseshoes, and boar's-head candlesticks. The palace park, one of the few high points in a level sandy area, offers a spectacular view of the bay of the Havel and the surrounding lakes, where the Glienecke Bridge connects Berlin and Potsdam. The view is very much as it was in August 1886 when Laforgue rented a boat to row around these royal sloping shores marked by "cannon of all dimensions, from those captured in wartime down to the royal toy cannon . . . and one that is fired at sunset every evening," and when he had been warned that months of prison would await him if he attempted to put in anywhere in the park. Of the landing that Laforgue describes welcoming the launch of William II, all that remains today are the stone steps in which the iron rings that once held the red carpet are still imbedded.

The militarism that the Prussian eagle symbolized had its genesis in the garrison town of Potsdam but reached its peak in the Field Marshals' Hall of the Kadetten Anstalt in Lichterfelde, to which Laforgue devotes his final chapter, describing in detail the reliefs by the sculptor Johannes Pfuhl (1846–1921) depicting scenes from the Franco-Prussian War. The Hall had been decorated to describe the historical development of the country and to extol the virtues of its commanders-in-chief. It displayed portraits of the Prussian kings, the German

Emperor, and the Field Marshals of the Prussian Army. But it was the scenes Pfuhl had created that drew Laforgue's attention, representing as they did the sentimental yet arrogant and sadistic nature of German character. The Kadetten Anstalt, which served as the West Point of the Prussian state and numbered among its graduates crown princes and many future generals including Hermann Goering, had been established in 1873 by William I. It ceased to operate as a military academy after World War I and in the 1930s detachments of Berlin police were stationed there. Hitler's private army of brown-shirted soldiers, the SA or Storm Troops, infiltrated the police and soon the barracks was for all practical purposes the headquarters of the Storm Troops. Thomas Blake describes what happened on June 30, 1934, when a "reorganization" conference was to take place at the Kadettenhaus: "About 65 of the high command arrived at the barracks to be 'briefed' on the new rules and regulations. Now the SS, who were formerly a security detachment within the SA, came into their own. As the leaders of the now doomed Storm Troops arrived for the conference they were met by armed squads of the SS and accused of participating in a plot to over-throw the German Government. Seventeen of those men were ultimately led to a wall at the corner of Basler Strasse and Finkensteinallee inside the compound where they were executed by SS firing squads. The shocked parliamentarians of the German Government were cowed into issuing an official telegram on the following Monday congratulating Hitler for saving the country from the so-called plot. The now dominant SS had also used the weekend to settle various personal scores. Leaders of the Catholic Action Group and several regular army generals and their wives were among the victims. The SS made the grounds and buildings their own and troops of the Fuehrer's personal bodyguard, Leibstandarte Adolf Hitler Regiment, were stationed at the site of their gruesome deed. Their black uniforms with the skull and crossbones insignia became a familiar and much-feared sight in the otherwise peaceful neighborhood." The buildings, badly damaged in the last weeks of World War II, subsequently became Andrews Barracks, headquarters for the United States Combat Support Battalion and Field Station personnel. Since the Wall came down, the buildings have reverted to Berlin municipal authorities, and whatever use they are now put to, it will certainly not be military.

Laforgue had ample time to explore Berlin and enjoy a varied life beyond the confines of the court. He made friends with the Ysaÿe brothers, Eugene, a violinist, and Théo, a pianist. Laforgue went regularly to Théo's room and would read or write while the pianist practiced. He also got to know the painters Max Klinger and Franz Skarbina, who did two portraits of him. He often went to the museums, the opera, the aquarium, the music halls, and the circus. He had a tempestuous affair with a woman to whom he refers in his agenda with the initial "R" (she was Rosa Bachem, the daughter of the mayor of Coblenz and Cologne, a lady-in-waiting at the court who was twenty years older than he).

Laforgue went to Berlin a decade after the disastrous defeat of the French at Sedan, and he was reminded at every moment in the newspapers, the beer gardens, and the music halls of the triumph of the German Army and of the proclamation of the Empire in the Hall of Mirrors at Versailles. Bismarck had exacted from the French an enormous indemnity of five billion francs. The influx of all this money led to a period of wild speculation, the so-called *Gründer- jahre*, during which everyone tried to make a fortune. The inevitable crash came in 1873, but it did little to slow Berlin's expansion. Real estate continued to boom; a hodge-podge of ugly apartment buildings was thrown up to the west in the districts of Schöneberg and Charlotten- burg and along the Kurfürstendamm, which Bismarck thought would one day rival the Champs Elysées. When it was completed it was only half as wide as its Parisian model and of- fered none of its broad vistas. "Chicago on the Spree," as Berlin was called, became the most American of cities. With its *nouveau riche* ve- neer, it resembled nothing so much as a big brash frontier town, and its society, as Laforgue observes, had the rough manners expected of one. Imperial Berlin was indeed American in spirit and his readers today will be struck by how much of this Berlin, more bad than good, has come down to us in modern America: the omnipresent beer, the heavy fattening food, the pictorial and architectural *kitsch* (it is no wonder that the word *kitsch* was coined in Germany), the tawdry and sentimental goods, especially the greeting cards, of the *Kaisergalerie*.

As I made my way around the ghost-city that Berlin has become, I felt everywhere the shades closing in on me. Jules Laforgue had brought me here and I sensed that he was next to me wherever I turned—in his room, on Unter den Linden and Friedrichstrasse, at the opera, in the beer halls, the museums, and at Babelsberg. Since I had known him for years, had read all his work and translated much of it, I found it reassuring to discover wherever I turned his moon-shaped face, his piercing blue-gray eyes, and the sensitive little build, the reserved, retiring presence, that he described so well in his *Hamlet*. The presence of Laforgue was indeed familiar but I soon realized that I had perhaps come in search of another young man of the same age whom I had once known far better—myself. For I had grown up in a milieu far from here that in many ways duplicated the atmosphere of the city Laforgue describes "in a slight state of siege." That was an army post, Jefferson Barracks, Missouri, just south of St. Louis, the first military post west of the Mississippi and still, in the 1920s and '30s when I knew it, one of the most important military posts in the country. My father was a professional soldier, a corporal in the Sixth Infantry Band, and I had witnessed, as had Laforgue, the constant clicking of heels, the snapping of salutes, the marching feet, the military regalia, the scraping of sabers along the hot pavement. The uniformed barracks, so tightly disciplined that one could scarcely breathe, was in every way a miniature imitation of the Prussian capital. The commanding officer, Colonel Walter Kreuger, had come from Prussia at an early age and had risen through the ranks of the United States Army. He was determined that the post he governed would equal in its spit and polish the military metropolis he had left behind. And indeed it did, and it was ready, as was he, when World War II arrived and he became one of the country's most important generals in the Pacific theatre. It was ironic that this Prussian concentration was situated at the heart of what had been a French enclave. Carondolet, adjacent to Jefferson Barracks, like St. Louis itself, had been founded by the French; its streets, its rivers, its neighborhoods all had French names. But its French aspect, along with that of the city, had been completely changed by the influx of Germans in the middle of the last century. They had brought their sense of law and order, their beer, their *gemütlichkeit*, their kindergarten (the one I attended was the first west of the Mississippi). It was their freshly scrubbed stone steps, their windows decorated with green porcelain pots of mother-in-law's tongue that I passed every morning on my way to school in South St. Louis. Having been born in Louisiana and loving everything French, I felt totally alienated from my Prussian military surroundings and my German beer-drinking city. That alienation was made all the stronger when the South St. Louis Germans, on the eve of World War II, in their organized beer-garden gatherings, became vociferous American supporters of Hitler and the Third Reich. I became convinced that Prussia might well produce a victorious army but that politically and socially it could only lead to total disaster.

"While all the others were boasting of how proudly the Prussian eagle soared toward the sun," wrote Heinrich Heine, "I prudently kept my eyes fixed upon its claws." And if I mention that I, too, was watching those claws much later and farther off, it is to show how long a shadow

Germany casts in the world and how important it is that a new Germany today emerge. Germany has always had a double nature. As Alson J. Smith puts it, "Germany is the classic case of national schizophrenia: . . . First there was (and is) the *gemütlich* Germany of the writers and artists and musicians; the learned Germany of the great universities and the pioneering scientists and the profound philosophers; the liberal and progressive Germany of the trade-union movements and the far-reaching systems of social security and insurance. Then there was (and is) the other Germany—the Germany that is restless when the drum beats; the Germany that, even in the midst of peace and good works, cannot help but lift its head at the distant sound of a bugle; the Germany in which the rhythmic stamp of jack-boots evokes an old, pre-Christian mystique of blood and iron and fierce Teutonic gods. This is the Germany that places order ahead of liberty, discipline ahead of creativity, pride and power ahead of intellectual and moral accomplishment, the Fatherland above the human race, *Deutschland uber alles!* This is Prussia's Germany, and Frederick the Great's, and Nietzsche's, and Wagner's. And this, oddly enough, is the romantic Germany, forever pur-

Schloss Sans Souci, Potsdam.

suing an illusion of God-given superiority and divine mission."

The world now is waiting to see which side of Germany will triumph and whether it has finally abandoned this illusion of its divine mission. The new German constitution, modeled on the American one, was written so that the horrors of the past would not be repeated, and great effort has been expended since World War II to build a truly democratic country. Certainly Prussian militarism seems a thing of the past. When in 1991 the remains of Frederick the Great, which during World War II had been removed to Bavaria for safe keeping, were returned and buried in a state ceremony beside his dogs at Sans Souci, Louis Ferdinand, the grandson of William I and head of the House of Hohenzollern, composed a funeral march for the occasion. Helmut Kohl was severely criticized for attending the ceremony, which for many underscored too strongly Prussia's militaristic past.

Anti-militarism among young Germans has grown to such an extent that the Bundeswehr has great difficulty filling its ranks. The problem is apparently particularly acute in Berlin, where Bernhard Steimle, director of the recruitment center, said recently, "The young people seem to think that military service is optional." And according to Matthias Mücke, leader of an anti-military group in Berlin, nearly half of the men of service age try to avoid the military. And it isn't hard for them to do so since ninety percent of the young Germans who apply to do civilian rather than military service have their wishes granted. Anti-military groups circulate samples of the sort of letter needed to be accepted for civilian service: "Even as a child I promised I would never hurt anyone" or "My mother forebade me to play war when I was little." A far cry, indeed, from the spirit of the young Prussian at the turn of the century. Dangerous militarism now seems to have shifted to the United States where lunatic militias, inspired by Nazi propaganda, are springing up nationwide.

Although Amnesty International in July 1994 warned that discrimination against minorities and brutal treatment of them in Germany was on the increase, the extreme right has been soundly defeated in recent elections. Ignatz Bubis, chairman of the Central Council of Jews in Germany, has said that while the youngest generation of Germans is definitely confronting the past, Jews in Germany are still not full-fledged citizens: "Germany is the only country where you hear talk of Germans and Jews. You would never hear anyone say 'Americans and Jews' in America. We Jews in Germany still live in our own ghettos. Even the official government term for us, 'Jewish fellow citizens,' excludes us. Why aren't we simply 'citizens'? For the great majority of Germans, a Jew is a foreigner, a stranger. My citizenship is in the papers every day. But the polls show that to fifty-seven percent of Germans, I am not a German citizen."

On V-E Day President Roman Herzog paid tribute to the generation of his parents for what it had accomplished after the war "in heaps of ruins and seas of blood." For him and others like him who were children, or not yet born, when the war ended, V-E Day represented, he said, neither defeat nor victory, but a door open on the future. Clearly there are vast empty areas in Berlin and in the rest of Germany that are, literally and psychologically, to be filled in, but it is to be hoped that in time that door will have swung wide open and the ugly German whom Laforgue delineates so distinctly in this book will be merely part of history.

I

ROYAL SUMMER RESIDENCES;
THE EMPEROR AND THE
EMPRESS AT THE STATION;
ENTRY INTO BERLIN

On a hot August afternoon I linger on the outskirts of Potsdam. On this plain stretching from Potsdam to Berlin, a sandy plain as marshy as the seashore, Potsdam, the Prussian Versailles, with its adjoining acres, is an oasis in which the Crown takes considerable pride.

Potsdam casts the shadows of its belltower and its barracks on one of those numerous lakes formed by the Havel. Ice-blue in color, these lakes lie side by side, surrounded by parks from which emerge the royal castles: Babelsberg, belonging to the Emperor, the Marble Palace to Prince William, his grandson, Glienicke to the son of the late Frederick Charles.[1] In a boat I rented in Potsdam I am making a tour of these famous shores. The man who rented me the boat carefully cautioned me about not putting in at any of the royal parks, and even led me to believe that months of prison would await me if I did. I drift along on my tour, edging as close to shore as the rushes permit. The silence of the oppressive afternoon hangs everywhere; two or three gulls come and go; swans sail by in formation. I make my way around the park of Babelsberg Castle. The Castle rises high above the trees; the flag indicating that the Emperor is in residence flies above it. Here and there, on the sloping shores, groups of cannon of all dimensions, from those captured in wartime down to the royal toy cannon; they are used for celebrations, and there is one that is fired at sunset every evening.

These clumps of trees are of that metallic and artificial green visible in the German landscape from the time of the Empire. And in fact all this oasis is somewhat artificial: one does not have to

---

[1] Prince Frederick Charles, the nephew of William I, died in 1885; his son Prince Frederick Leopold owned Glienecke at this time.

dig very far down with one's cane to find sand; and I have just passed a pump house where a powerful apparatus starts pumping water across the park at six o'clock every morning.

It is three o'clock, the time of siesta. In half an hour, the Emperor and the Empress will sit down with their guests. During their month's stay at Babelsberg,[2] every party includes some distinguished visitor.

The only human faces I have seen have been those of gaunt, ragged peasants, men and women, sweeping a path. But now down the path that skirts the shore comes a patrol of six foot soldiers. The leader, holding his rifle under one arm with the barrel to the ground, signals me to keep farther away.

I turn my boat farther off shore. I come upon a little sailboat in which there is a good German fellow in shirtsleeves with his wife. The husband works the sail, and in the bottom of the boat is a keg of beer. I start back toward Potsdam. A barge loaded with a mountain of fodder goes slowly past. There on the bank, some hussars in red uniforms come down to water their horses. A narrow canal, lake and rushes again,

[2] Routinely twenty days; see below, p. 104.

another canal lined with quais and I am in town, where the only sound is the click of spurs on the old stone. The Castle and its park are but a step away, and I go there for a breath of air. At the Garrison Church a clock strikes the hour and then the bells ring out to the tune of an old German hymn which says:

> *Go always loyal and true*
> *To thy cold tomb,*
> *And turn not aside*
> *From the path of the Lord.*[3]

The bells ring thus every half hour. Meager distraction; the boredom one feels is ineffable. But Berlin is only forty minutes away.

I go by coach as far as Neu-Babelsberg. The road is bordered by overhanging trees during the greater part of the journey; and later by poor ramshackle houses. From the complexions of the tow-headed peasants one sees, especially women and children, one can guess the principal item of nourishment—potatoes. I can't help thinking of those villages, on the edge of Versailles, where Madame de Maintenon went in

[3]The hymn is by Ludwig Heinrich Christoph Hölty (1748–76), the author of sentimental religious lyrics.

the company of her favorite from St. Cyr, to distribute bread, clothing, and alms.

Some of the court coaches go by, simple barouches, manned by coachmen and footmen in black uniforms with aiguillettes and silver trimming. The coachmen and footmen at court never grow moustaches, which is a curious protest (of English and French origin) against the Berlin domestics who grow beards, and especially moustaches, to their liking.

The dinner party is over. I meet two stiff figures in full dress, riding together in the same barouche. As Berliners commonly put it, they are certainly "not from these parts." These gentlemen are the Duke of Sagan[4] and Count Guillaume de Pourtalès; the former, small and laughable in his typical Restoration dress, happy to lead a court life and to move about in uniform on social occasions; the latter, the proud remains of a rounder whose imposing bald head and long white beard allow him to pose in court charades as an old pilgrim, a great Magyar lord,

[4]Louis de Talleyrand-Périgord (1811–98), the fourth Duke of Sagan. Sagan (today Zagan), a city in Silesia in Poland, capital of the ancient principality of Sagan. The title Duke of Sagan had passed in 1862 to the family of Talleyrand-Périgord.

and other such subjects, happy also to lead a court life and to wear at dress balls a superb unidentifiable red costume. The Duke—with his Duchess, grand-daughter of Marshal Castellane—and the Count are the great resources, as far as conversation goes, of the teas over which the Empress presides.

A little farther along, in another carriage, the famous Marquess of Tseng with some Chinese from the Embassy smoking cigarettes and chatting in their exotic and cunning way. (Much is said of Chinese politeness; I was to discover the following morning that, as soon as everyone got up from table, the Marquess and his Chinese companions made unceremoniously for the door, and the Lord Chamberlain, Count Perponcher, shouted to them from the far end of the table: "Hold on, Gentlemen. You did not say good day to the Emperor. As a Chinaman, you may pass, but certainly not as a Marquess!")

As I cross the Glienicke Bridge[5] over a nar-

[5]The present elegant iron suspension bridge, built in 1908–9, replaces the Glienicke Bridge of Laforgue's time, a monumental Neo-classical structure designed by Schinkel. Spanning two small lakes, the Jungfernsee and the Tiefer See, it lies on the boundary between Berlin and Potsdam. After the construction of the Wall, the German Democratic

row channel connecting two lakes between Potsdam and the still-deserted Palace of the late Frederick Charles, my carriage is forced to stop, along with a number of pedestrians. The gates on the central arch of the bridge are raised in order to let a barge pass with a mountain of fodder. When the mountain has gone by, the gates are again lowered, but the pedestrians continue to wait and others come to join them. My coachman signals that we also must wait. Alongside the landing (nothing but a plank) of Babelsberg Castle, arrives a luxurious launch. Between the coxswain and the two sailors in white at the oars is seated a red-uniformed hussar officer, covered with medals. The people in the crowd remove their hats, the officer salutes. This is Prince William, the Emperor's grandson, who is returning home to the Marble Palace, and in such fine weather prefers his launch to his carriage.

At this time the next afternoon, in the same hot sun, I stand on the same baked and crack-

Republic renamed the bridge Brucke der Einheit (Unity Bridge). It was familiarly known in the West as the "Bridge of Spies." On it in 1962 Colonel Rudolph Abel, the Russian spy, was exchanged for Lieutenant Gary Powers, whose U2 plane had been shot down over the Soviet Union. And it was across this bridge that Anatoly B. Shcharansky, the Russian Jewish dissident, walked to freedom in 1985.

ing earth near the little railroad station of Neu-
Babelsberg. A special train, made up of the
Empress's special blue saloon car and some first-
and second-class coaches, awaits the sovereigns.
After the routine twenty-day period, Their
Majesties are leaving the Castle of Babelsberg
for Berlin. The big military parade takes place
tomorrow morning. Day after tomorrow is the
anniversary of Sedan.[6]

The stationmaster has put on his fine cap and
his string of decorations. A few footmen in undress livery are already waiting around. Carriages are arriving one by one. Two doctors, one
in uniform, the Emperor's, and the other, in
civilian clothes, the Empress's. Three or four
quartermasters, a baggagemaster, in dustcoats;
our lowest employee wouldn't own their anti-
quated, faded top hats nor their shapeless shoes.
All these people seem rigidly disciplined and
quite unaccustomed to the civilities of court life.

Finally we have a real personage: an old
dandy with overly waxed moustaches, stiff and
formal in a suit that comes neither from Paris
nor London. His top hat needs a few strokes of

[6]Sedan, in northeastern France near the Belgian border, was
the scene (1870) of the decisive French defeat in the Franco-
Prussian War and of the capture of Napoleon III.

the iron (ah, the top hats, all the top hats one sees in Germany!). This is the Lord Chamberlain of the Palace, Count Perponcher, who occupies the highest position at the court. We shall meet him again in all the glory of his functions. The Count has at his side a young relative, a Guard officer, a baron, a budding Chamberlain.

Neither Countess Perponcher, Mistress of the Robes, nor Countess Hacke, Mistress of the Bedchamber, is here. The Empress has with her only two ladies, Countess Oriola, permanent lady-in-waiting who lives at the palace and receives a salary, and one of the many young provincial countesses who rotate from month to month in a sort of apprenticeship, when the Empress is in the country.

People line up and remove their hats. Their Majesties arrive together in the Empress's open carriage, a vehicle with a square, extremely low body, in which the Empress may be installed in the very chair in which she is rolled across her apartments.[7] The Emperor, with lowered head, smiling his happy, feeble, finished smile beneath a constantly curled moustache, is seated as if collapsed, two white gloved hands poised on

[7]The Empress had been confined to a wheelchair since 12 August 1882 when she slipped and fell at Babelsberg.

his knees. He is in undress, slightly worn, uniform, and wears a simple cap, one of remarkably modest height in contrast to those adopted recently by Berlin's elegant officers.

The Empress has on a black dress ornamented with black beads. She wears black only for journeys and court mourning. At all other times she does not hesitate to don the liveliest colors, which framing her thin hunched body and her proud wrinkled and painted face, make her the most extraordinary character of whom a Talleyrand or a Lord Beaconsfield could ever have dreamt, and whom Herr von Bismarck, who is neither a Talleyrand nor a Beaconsfield, has not found to his German liking.

Accompanied by the Chamberlain, the two sovereigns, bowed with age, make their way slowly toward the saloon car. Footmen help them to mount. The stationmaster salutes as the train pulls out.

On its arrival at the Potsdam station in Berlin, the square in front of the station, which is the busiest and most central point in the city, will be cleared by policemen on horseback holding back the curious spectators. And there will be another uninterrupted line of guards on horseback and two compact rows of good Berliners

the whole length of Unter den Linden as far as
the Imperial Palace, on which the flag announcing the Emperor's residence in Berlin will already be unfurled.

Entry into the Prussian capital by rail is cold
and dreary. It is not like arriving in Paris after
having passed gay country houses and gardens,
typical Parisian suburbs, followed by those districts with tall buildings covered with posters,
billboards and flowering balconies, all swarming with people and shops, on both sides of the
noisy operations of the station. Here the country
consists of nothing but sand, with dark pine
trees on both sides of the track; and then one
comes suddenly on the highways leading into
the city, and low houses daubed with that potato or macadam color so characteristic of the local scene. No billboards, balconies, or shutters
break the monotony. On the street level there are
steps leading down into shops. One must see
these houses to understand how sinister a façade
without balconies and especially without shutters (which gives the windows the appearance
of mere holes) can be; and to appreciate the
real beauty of the façade of an ordinary house in
Paris.

It is twilight, a late August twilight. In the

station, in fourth-class railway carriages, workmen are taking their places. Their dress aston-
ishes one: instead of blouses, smocks, or blue
trousers they wear greasy threadbare dustcoats
and visored caps; and their dishevelled hair and
heavy beards make them look strangely like gal-
ley slaves.

German stations do not have a look of old
stone as do ours in Paris; they are all new, airy,
built in Trocadero style of red brick or sand-
stone, always quite ornate. Above all, they are
light and spacious, intended more for traffic
than for sheltering a maze of offices. The employees are veritable soldiers in uniform; with
their heels together, they stand stiffly at attention
and salute their chiefs.

It is amusing to notice the contrast in dress
between the German and French employees on
the border at German Avricourt and French
Avricourt.[8] On one side you find military personnel going quietly about the business of the
station exactly as they did yesterday and the day
before. On the other, as soon as you arrive, there
is a slight odor of absinthe and freedom, with

[8] Avricourt in Lorraine was at the time on the Franco-
German border because Alsace-Lorraine had been annexed
by Germany after the defeat of France in 1870.

employees who drag their feet or appear to do so since they have no understraps to their gaiters, whistling (whistling!) calling to one another: "Will I see you tonight?" etc. With or without tickets, the public is free to move at will in German stations.

The station of the worst subprefecture in France would have a better restaurant than you find in any Berlin station.

2

IMPRESSIONS OF
THE MONARCHY AND
THE ARMY; MILITARIA

Berlin is called the "metropolis of the Empire"; it is also frequently called *die Kaiserstadt*, the Emperor's city.

Most shops add to their signboards the title of *Hoflieferant*, "supplier to the court." This title is accompanied by an enormous gilded shield with the arms of Prussia flanked by two naked Hercules with clubs. Some are more detailed. A piano merchant is "supplier by special appointment to Her Highness the Princess Frederick Charles"; a cigar merchant is "supplier by special appointment to His Imperial and Royal Highness the Crown Prince"; and there is the dentist by special appointment to Prince Frederick Charles, who died not long ago; the pho-

Bismarck. Kiel.

tographer by special appointment to the Emperor; the milliner by special appointment to the Empress.[1]

There are busts of the Emperor and the Crown Prince in all Berlin restaurants, in all beer halls, and in the open stands where Seltzer water is sold. There are chromo portraits of Bismarck and von Moltke, the "paladins" of the Emperor.

In a music shop window there are, of course, photographs of Rubinstein, Liszt, Joachim, Wagner—but among these photographs there are also—as a matter of course—those of the Emperor, Prince William, and Bismarck.

One photograph much in demand these days is one showing a baby, the Emperor's great-grandson, with a small cannon at his feet and near him a helmet on a chair.

There is in the window of the music shop to which I have referred a waltz entitled *Hohenzollern-Wetter* ("Hohenzollern weather"), that is, fine weather. When it is fine, people say here:

[1] In like fashion the British Ratting Company of East Grinstead, which caught rats at the Queen of England's Sandringham estate, was in 1958 entitled to display the royal crest with the words: "By Appointment, Suppliers to H. M. the Queen."

this is "Emperor's weather," just as they say in London, "Queen's weather."

There are, along Unter den Linden, displays of photographs all devoted to the court. Here is the family of the Crown Prince skating, with his aide-de-camp and ladies-in-waiting; there, a group of hunters in the snow, the Crown Prince, his pipe in his mouth, Prince William, Minister Puttkamer,[2] and the Russian Ambassador Count Schouvaloff; farther on, grouped on a castle cornerstone, Bismarck's family dressed for a wedding with the wedding couple in the foreground; farther on, the young princesses, the Crown Prince's daughters, in historic costumes; finally, in their plush frames mounted with the crowns of dukes and counts, gold-striped chamberlains, guard officers, Princess George Radziwill,[3] and others.

In a bookseller's window, I notice a poem in several cantos entitled *William, the Unique*, also the *Book of Queen Louise* and the *Travels of Prince Henry Around the World*; the cover of the lat-

[2] Robert von Puttkamer, the reactionary Minister of the Interior, was forced to resign by Frederick III, but returned to power after the latter's death.

[3] Princess George Radziwill (née Maria-Rosa Branicki) was the daughter-in-law of the Emperor's aide-de-camp Prince Anton Radziwill.

ter bears a colored engraving representing the young prince standing in a boat, saluting amid cannon smoke.

A spectacle more than monarchic, Asiatic one might say, may be enjoyed once or twice a week, on Unter den Linden and in the neighboring streets. A few passers-by remove their hats, draw back and bow: followed by a few urchins, Prince George,[4] a solitary Tiberius, who is never seen at court and who has written a *Phaedra* for Sarah Bernhardt, strolls along in his general's uniform, slow, bloated, with a most unwholesome look. On very high springs, finely balanced, his carriage follows him. He enters the shops and especially, quite boldly, into those on Friedrichstrasse that sell every sort of photograph. When he is weary, he motions to his carriage to draw near; the footman holds his general's coat with its red facings: he mounts amid the gaping throng, and rides off, finely balanced, in pursuit of his pleasures.

The Opera and the Royal Theatre (*Schauspielhaus*) are the property of the Emperor. Before putting up a poster, they consult the sover-

[4] Prince George of Prussia (1826–1902), grandson of Frederick William II, wrote a number of dramas under the name of G. Conrad.

eign. If he has chosen a play, the poster bears at the top: *Auf allerhöchsten Befehl* ("By order of the Emperor"). If the Crown Prince has chosen the play, the poster says only *Auf höchsten Befehl*. On the days of military parades, the public is virtually driven from the Opera: the Emperor places three-fourths of the seats at the disposal of the army and serves up a prodigious ballet. Frederick the Great posted a grenadier beside recalcitrant singers and thus forced them to perform. A year ago the most talented singer of the Opera, Fraulein Lehmann, as the result of a disagreement, broke her contract and left Berlin: since then, the daily poster bears at the bottom: *Fraulein Lehmann contraktbruchig* ("Fraulein Lehmann broke her contract"). In 1884, in the midst of a concert, the pianist von Bülow called the Berlin Opera the "Hülsen Circus" (Herr von Hülsen[5] is the manager of the Royal Theatres). Herr von Hülsen had Herr von Bülow's photograph distributed to all his employees so that this insulter might never be allowed to enter the theatre. Last January Herr von Bülow

[5]Botho von Hülsen, who died in 1886. A former lieutenant of the guard, he had been named manager of the Royal Theatres by Frederick William IV and had run them with military efficiency. He was the *bête noire* of the Wagnerians because he seldom produced Wagnerian operas.

happened to appear for the première of *Merlin*; an employee immediately asked him to leave and reimbursed him for his ticket.

MILITARIA: I find myself before a mailbox with an ordinary soldier; after my letter he posts an enormous envelope. I can't make out the address; the envelope is not stamped but has at the bottom a word in huge letters sticking out a mile: "MILITARIA," that is, "Military Affairs"—do not touch, this is sacred!

Noon in Berlin is the high point of the day, when the relieving guard, led by its band, passes before the Emperor's Palace. The fifes shrill those thin monotonous tunes that Berlin urchins whistle as they stroll about. Nearing the Palace, on a signal from the standard bearer, the fifes stop and the band begins to play. The standard, which precedes the band, is rather strange. Imagine a silver star surmounted by a spread eagle: above the eagle, a Chinese hat with its little bells supporting a crescent, from the tips of which hang two horse-hair tassels, one red, the other, white. They arrive at the Palace. The soldiers mark time and all twist their necks in the direction of the corner window, the "historic window." The Emperor appears at this window,

in a white waistcoat, a red-lapelled tunic, the
Cross Pour le Mérite around his neck, the 1870
Cross on his chest. He smiles; and is acclaimed
by shouts of approval and the lifting of hundreds of hats. The high point, the military high
point of the day, is over.

In Paris we have only the cannon at the Palais-
Royal on sunny days.

The principal change of guard is that of the
Honor Guard. The Royal Guard House is truly
the moral and symbolic center of Berlin, just as
it is the geographic center. Planted in the middle
of Unter den Linden, between the University
and the Arsenal (museum), facing the two Palaces and the Opera, it is a sort of Roman *cas-
trum*, a low gray temple with a triangular pediment with bas-reliefs preceded by a portico of
six columns. The whole structure is surrounded
by an iron railing. In front, between the iron
railing and the portico are two parallel rows of
twenty pickets, each furnished with a gun-rest.
These pickets mark each soldier's place and fa-
cilitate his falling into line. I should add that
small and insignificant as they are, they are
painted in the colors of Prussia, like the sentry-
boxes. Our sentry-boxes are tricolor only since

the days of Minister Boulanger.[6] To the last of these pickets is attached a drum, the little flat Prussian drum that resounds so dryly. A sentry is posted there near the railing. He does not stride up and down since he must keep a sharp lookout to the right and left of the avenue. As soon as a court carriage appears—most often a simple brougham whose coachman with his aiguillettes and silver-braided cap can be seen from afar—if the coachman holds his whip in a way that means that the carriage is occupied, the guard turns toward the portico, brings his hand to his mouth and shouts, *Raus!* (abbreviated form of *Heraus*—"Out!").

At once the foot soldiers rush forward down the steps. In the twinkling of an eye the two rows line up, shoulder arms, the drummer hooks his instrument to his belt, drumsticks at his side, and the officer, at the end, stands ready to present his sword.

A carriage passes. *Raus!* The guardsmen present arms, the officer salutes and the drum taps a rat-a-tat-tat of honor. In the carriage are two nurses holding two royal babies on their laps.

[6]General Georges Boulanger was named French Defense Minister in 1886.

The drum is played only for the royal family: for a general only half the guardsmen come forward.

April, 9:00 A.M. —Everything, even the gray Guard House, shines in the sunlight. The soldiers are warming themselves outside as they lean on the columns, polished and sparkling, neither awkward nor ungainly, three fourths clean-shaven, seeming happy to be there, in the Berlin sunlight. With their hands in their pockets or their arms crossed, they chat with one another. Urchins, hanging on the bars, are watching them, waiting for the passing of some royal carriage in order to see them come to attention. The tips of the helmets and the buttons of the tunics sparkle; no gloves. The officer, with his silver belt and enormous tassels falling to his side, strides up and down. Sparrows nest and play in the bas-reliefs of the pediment.

Orders. There is on the left of the Royal Guard House a space planted with several large trees containing two enormous cannon taken from the French in 1814. There, on certain days, once a week, I believe, officers come to receive their orders. Seen from a second floor, the spectacle is marvelous, especially when the day falls on a Sunday or a feast day and the army is in full dress. A military band plays in the center. The row of policemen is augmented by the orderlies who have accompanied their officers: the orderlies' helmets are topped with white, red, black falling horsetails. Ordinary officers have the same horsetail as ordinary soldiers. The ranking officers wear on the tips of their helmets a floating bouquet of long black or white plumes. The officers arrive. The wealthy officer steps down from his private carriage, the poor officer pays for his cab. They enter the circle. One then has a unique spectacle, a moving floor of color and glitter, animated by the same rhythmic gesture, the German salute—nothing but bowing torsos, hands smartly raised and lowered, with, of course, the three steps forward that precede the salute. There are officers of every unit and of every color. The one who dominates everything and is the cynosure of all eyes is the guard officer, a giant fellow dressed all in white and wearing a helmet of clear metal topped by a silver spread eagle. The crowd never ceases to stand in awe of him, although well aware of his vanity.

On Sundays and feasts days and holidays because of the return from church and the constant coming and going among the various palaces, the guardsmen are kept permanently between their pickets.

Eight o'clock one winter morning. Below my window, young officers of different units march past in groups of two or three. A pretty spectacle, neat and clean, a real picture-book procession. It is cold; all of them have raised their coat collars, which looks quite nice, the coat being completely black, except that the underside of this collar is the color of the cap-cord. I couldn't possibly list all the colors. There is a blue cap with a canary-yellow cord, a black cap with a red cover (the most usual one), a blue cap with a black velvet cord, a black cap with a currant-colored cord (headquarters corps), a white cap with a vermilion cord (Guardsmen). Only the color of the cap and the underside of the collar change: the rest is fixed: black coat, long black greatcoat, black trousers.

At the intersection of Unter den Linden and Friedrichstrasse, the most crowded point in Berlin, I pause one summer afternoon. And dazed momentarily, as if dreaming, I pick out what I take to be the chief traffic noise; it turns out in reality to be a saber dragging the ground.

Officers wear their uniforms even when going to small theatres.

At the circus, on days when the horses are exercised, young military aristocrats crowd into the boxes, and then during intermission drag their sabers off toward the stables, before the bowing circus personnel.

Friedrichstrasse, barely twilight; two soldiers have stopped to chat with a maid—as in Paris they might, say, in the rue de Richelieu. An officer arrives. The maid quickly steps back; the two soldiers come to attention, salute, their eyes fixed on the officer as he moves on.

This fashion in saluting, of meeting the officer's gaze four steps before he arrives, of fixing him with the eye and following him with the same intense stare, for four more steps until he has passed, is often irresistibly grotesque. No less comic are the young cadets of ten or twelve years of age, striding down Unter den Linden of a Sunday, meeting and stiffly saluting one another.

Military dress has the greatest influence on the dress of those elegant young gentlemen in Berlin who care about how they look. I shall give details later. The chief characteristic is naturally the main one of a soldier's bearing, the stiffness, and with that, the measured step, and often, indeed, very often, the mania of clicking the heels. Everyone in Berlin, no matter what the current fashion, wears heels that are extremely high. With regard to the furious tapping with the soles of the feet in what is here called the march step and the reason for which seems so unclear, an officer tells me that this step is the best exercise for breaking in a soldier. And he adds that in 1871, around Paris, at the very moment of the siege, the crippling effect of the whole campaign and the joyous anticipation of a return home had weakened the discipline of the troops. The officers then had recourse to the march step, with knees braced, several hours a day with immediate results.

The military salute has gone over completely into civilian life. Go out early in the morning and you will see ordinary civilian employees, meeting others whom they know, bring their hands nonchalantly to their foreheads to salute and say: "*Morgen . . . Morgen . . .* Good morning, Good morning . . ." I have even seen an old family landau pull up before the Opera. The coachman was an ordinary servant in a faded top hat and coat. (Whenever anyone gets in or out of a court carriage, the coachman, of course, brings up his hand to salute.) The family got out of this carriage and the decrepit old coachman brought his hand to his forehead and did not bring it down until the last family member had disappeared behind the door.

German families, as we know, print their wedding announcements and other intimate details of their lives on the back pages of the newspapers. But officers announce their engagements only in the *Neue Preussische Zeitung*, a much-favored paper, among more or less contrasting advertisements.

And with all this magnificent military deployment, Berlin lives and breathes in a slight state of siege.

3

THE COURT

The first entertainment of the year given by the Emperor and the Empress is a concert at the Royal Palace (the *Schloss*) attended only by the diplomatic corps and the court. In several rows the ambassadors and their wives sit chatting (in the very middle of the front row is the wife of the French Ambassador). The court is expected at any moment; the singers are ready. The court enters, the diplomatic corps gets up and sits back down only after the court is seated, on several rows of armchairs opposite the diplomatic corps. Everything is quite solemn: people sit down, look at one another, the concert begins.

Here we have the Emperor, wearing the uniform of a general, sunk deep in his chair, exchanging from time to time a few words with the Crown Princess, who sits beside him, youthful and gay. The Empress has remained away as usual. Prince Frederick Charles has not come. Prince William enjoys a joke with his wife and his sister Princess Victoria about some singer's looks. The Crown Prince is sad. The Empress's two ladies-in-waiting and her Mistress of the Robes are seated in the second row. The aides-de-camp and the chamberlains stand in the rear.

There is an intermission during which the court and the diplomatic corps mingle discreetly, "making a circle" as it is called. Then the concert resumes.

Here we have almost the entire court; it is not a very sizeable one, even with the officers and the ladies-in-waiting attached to it; but if all the Hohenzollerns living, from the Emperor down to his last great-grandson, were brought together, they would, as everyone knows, make quite a respectable family.

The Emperor is rich; the court, according to tradition, remains poor; the salaries are ridiculously low; not a shred of comfort has been introduced into the Palace.

No etiquette: when presented to one or the

other of the sovereigns you simply nod your head, and wait to be addressed. The Empress is always delighted to hear herself called "Madam."

Palace life functions with an immutable monotony. Every hour upstairs (with the Empress) or downstairs (with the Emperor) is taken care of. The two live apart. How quiet the Palace is when at dusk the Emperor is in his study and the Empress with her ladies-in-waiting! Only the voices of the footmen in the front hall, the ticking of clocks, water dripping on the palm leaves in the little conservatory—then suddenly the bell rings, the door opens, and there is the click of spurs as a guard enters and removes a paper from his helmet.

From the first of December to the first of May, the Emperor and Empress occupy the Imperial Palace in Berlin. In the summer they are at Coblenz, Baden-Baden, Ems, Hamburg, or Wiesbaden in castles of varying comfort or in small hotels, when no castles are available. At Baden-Baden, for example, which is their favorite villeggiatura and the only one where the two sovereigns live together more or less as they do in Berlin, they inhabit a hotel separated only by a courtyard with fountain and flowerbed

from an annex occupied by ordinary travelers.[1]
From the windows of this annex, one can easily
follow Their Majesties in their apartments and
be present at many of the less solemn details of
their existence.

The Imperial Palace in Berlin is situated
at the center of Unter den Linden. It adjoins
an eighteenth-century-style library and is itself
constructed in that heavy, cold Greek style
which Berlin architects have not yet entirely
abandoned for a return to German Renaissance.
The exterior is painted in that dull grayish tan
that is found almost everywhere, and that to the
new arrival seems to be the dominant tone of the
capital. Across the façade is a portico of four columns with two winding ramps for carriages;
from its flat roof a flag is hoisted when the Emperor is in residence. The Palace is very small;
there is just one floor wide enough to allow for
thirteen windows. Only the Emperor, the Empress, and the Empress's four or five attendants
live here. The rest of the court lives at the Royal
Palace (the *Schloss*), which is ten minutes away,
at the Prinzessinnen-Palais five minutes away,
or at the Palace of the Netherlands, but a step
away, that is, of course, those who are unmar-

[1] Hotel Messmer; Laforgue stayed in the annex.

ried. For the Empress has very definite ideas on the subject, and will not permit a palace of hers to house a couple of any sort. The Imperial Palace is divided in two, the left wing is given over to the sovereigns' private apartments, the Emperor on the ground floor, the Empress on the second floor; the right wing is taken up with reception and entertainment rooms. The large rooms are furnished in Empire style, some of them serving as museums for the silver brought by national delegations, one for the presents from China and Japan. The private apartments have gradually filled to overflowing with an odd assortment of rather inelegant Christmas presents; the large number of marble vases and little modern tables and chairs is especially deplorable. On the other hand, the only paintings to be seen are in a small room on the ground floor where the Empress serves tea. The Emperor, who never visits a museum or an exhibition, buys up a stock of mediocre canvases every season; these are subsequently distributed throughout the halls and castle rooms that are inhabited for only one month a year. The halls of the Palace are adorned indiscriminately with ordinary plaster figures. The stairway is decorated with three huge allegorical statues by

Rauch,[2] the official sculptor of the last reign. We might mention in passing that the Palace of the Crown Prince provides a happy contrast to these poor and tasteless furnishings, thanks especially to the artistic care of the Princess Royal.

The principal room in the Emperor's private apartment is his study. One of the windows in this room, looking out on Unter den Linden, is known throughout Germany as the *historische Eck-Fenster*, because it is at this window, located at the very corner of the palace, that the Emperor shows himself to the crowd every day at noon, when the Guard files by.[3] Through this same window at night the passerby can see, by the light of a little lamp, the head of the Emperor bent over his desk. The study is adorned with family portraits and military souvenirs; on a table is a bouquet of his favorite cornflowers which is changed each morning. In this room the sovereign receives his Chancellor, Prince von Bismarck, and confers with him.

The Empress's apartment contains, in addi-

[2]Christian Daniel Rauch (1777–1857), representative of the Berlin school of Neo-classical sculpture. His best-known piece is the equestrian statue of Frederick the Great on Unter den Linden.
[3]The Emperor stood with such regularity at this window that the event was recorded in the Baedeker guide to Berlin.

tion to her private rooms, several small drawing rooms for private receptions or audiences. They are, in general, decorated with an indiscriminate luxury and filled with Christmas presents. No library; the Empress has her library in the Castle at Coblenz; here, nothing but ornate illustrated books, most of which are annual presents from Queen Victoria of England. A small piano that has been quiet for some time. Between the Empress's apartment and the large ballrooms is a little conservatory, well kept but commonplace with its spreading palm branches supporting polychrome china parrots.

The Palace contains no bathroom whatever, strange as that may seem.[4]

The domestic personnel of the Palace is limited in number, and although fundamentally well disciplined, displays an unbelievable lack of training. There are moments in fact when none of the half dozen footmen whose duty it is to move about in the front hall is at his post, and when one could enter the Palace and find himself suddenly confronting the Emperor and Empress. It has been known to happen.

---

[4]When the Emperor wished to bathe, a wooden tub was brought over from the Grand Hôtel de Rome at 39 Unter den Linden.

4

THE EMPEROR

For the historian William I, King of Prussia, Emperor of Germany,[1] is indeed the least complicated of characters. Has he a passion, a marked taste, a mania? No. He is neither a literary man nor an utterer of historic *bon mots* like his predecessor; he is not artistic like so many of his satellite princelings today; he is neither devout nor a free-thinker; neither a gourmand nor a drinker: above all, he is a soldier, but not an old trooper.

William I will have done nothing to leave a legend behind him. As king, he wanted only to

[1] William I (1797–1888) was King of Prussia 1861–88 and German Emperor 1871–88; he married Maria Luisa Augusta Catherina of Saxe-Weimar on June 11, 1829.

Emperor William I.
Schloss Charlottenburg Mausoleum, Berlin.

be an "irreproachable watchman," all he has had to do is leave things alone, and every summer, when he enters Ems or Homburg, he passes under the triumphal arches of foliage where inscriptions greet him with a name that history (German history at least) will keep for him: "To William the Victorious."

Through so many triumphs and so many upheavals he has not turned aside from the good bourgeois life of his years of adolescence and poverty. Here he is having reached, without any malady except old age, the majestic culmination of ninety, brimming with the faith that Providence still needs him and that he is in Europe today the Good Shepherd of his people, the dispenser of peace.

When one is presented to His Majesty, his first glance takes your measure: foot soldier? cavalryman? dragoon? his glance seems to inquire mechanically. One is confronted by a superb cuirassier, tightly laced in a black, red-trimmed uniform, in no way deformed by age, scarcely stooped. The Berlin public would have it that thanks only to a stiff corset can their sovereign stand straight. The Emperor wears nothing of the sort: his only armor is the almost secular habit of parade and discipline. His face is extraordinarily lined and shrivelled; he looks pained, but he smiles and it is with a gesture, neither overly gallant nor senile, that the old soldier twists, as he speaks, the ends of his white moustache.

The Emperor utters only short sentences, with firmness and at the same time with the almost surly stammer of old soldiers who prefer stout handshakes to fine talk. The Emperor knows French passably well, but he has never had much pretention about it, and now for some time, he has had to utter no more than formal phrases in that language. He knows English better, as a result of his forced stay in England, at the time of the events of 1848,[2] a stay that the exiled prince used profitably to study a bit and complete, especially in history, his education, which was always far from brilliant.

The Emperor has never been a scholar; science, like art, is absolutely closed to him: he is

[2]"The revolutionary whirlwind that swept through Europe in 1848 reached Berlin in March and King Frederick Wilhelm IV, losing his nerve in the face of a threatening mob, granted Prussia a constitution. . . . Prince Wilhelm, though disagreeing with his brother's capitulation to the wishes of the mob, was in no position to do anything about it: considered to be the personification of hated autocracy (the 'grapeshot Prince' they called him) Wilhelm had been forced to flee for his life." *The Kaisers*, p. 15.

not even interested in German literature. He has read only one French novel, *The Wandering Jew* of Eugène Sue. There are on his table nothing but booklets concerning the army, and every week he leafs through the pictures of the *Illustration*, the *Graphic*, and the *London News*. Neither the Emperor nor Bismarck, Moltke and all his generation of heroes has ever been seen in a museum; and last summer there was the greatest difficulty, up to the last minute, to get him to open the Exhibition of Fine Arts in Berlin, celebrating the centenary of Berlin "Salons." The Emperor never goes to a concert. Wagner fought on the barricades in 1848, and that is forgotten, but to be a Wagnerian like his grandson Prince William, who calls Bayreuth "the new Olympus," or like his minister Herr von Puttkamer, is, in his eyes, slightly mad. Drama and comedy scarcely interest him; the opera is his only distraction; he rarely ever misses a ballet, and, on the evening of the parades, he gives over three-fourths of the seats in the theatre to the officers in Berlin and offers them a prodigious ballet.

The Emperor's voice is a good thick military one, sympathetic and serious, laced with firm and loyal intonations, with something fatalistic and mystical about it. Even today, in official ceremonies, the old sovereign's voice carries better than his son's, which is a bit thin and breathless.

I have called that voice mystical and fatalistic. And hearing it, one almost has a sense that his entire character and his life are revealed. Picture a prince reared in the turmoil of the Napoleonic wars, brought up in an impoverished court, coming to the throne at the age of sixty, and then, urged on by an insurmountable instinct of weakness to hang on, against everyone's advice, to a paradoxical turbulent, terrorizing minister, who falls upon him like a meteor and whose character is just the opposite of his.[3] Picture him throwing himself every evening on his knees to ask God's advice, cursing this "tyrant," this "despot," who pushes him into the "fratricidal" war of 1866,[4] who makes his subjects no longer salute him in the streets, who pushes him above

[3]Otto von Bismarck (1815–98), the "Iron Chancellor." In 1862 he was appointed Chancellor and Foreign Minister of Prussia and in 1871 became the first Chancellor of the German Empire, which he had helped create. Even after his dismissal by William II in 1890, he remained popular in Berlin.

[4]"On 3 July 1866, three weeks after the outbreak of hostilities, the Austrians were decisively defeated at the battle of Sadowa. King Wilhelm, who had had to be coerced into tak-

75

all to the most sensitive extremity that a soul imbued with legitimacy may have: the loss of Hanover, Saxony, Würtemberg, Mecklenburg. And giving in even further to this despot, being finally led, after a series of unprecedented triumphs, to avenge his mother for the impertinences of Napoleon I, assuming again at Versailles the old title of German Emperor, to become finally the European patriarch whom the poets of the German press today celebrate.

"By the grace of God,"—that turn of phrase is, in the mouth of William I, more than a traditional expression of the throne; one must remember that he thanks Providence at the beginning of all his war communiqués. William the Victorious is certainly of all Germans, and especially all Prussians, the one whom these recent prodigious events have marked with the least arrogance. Not only before Europe and the German public, but also before his intimate palace associates and in his less official moments, the sovereign likes to state "that it was

ing up arms against his fellow Germans, was delighted by the victory and it was with the utmost difficulty that Bismarck (who realized that Prussia had to be magnanimous) was able to restrain him from pushing on to Vienna." *The Kaisers*, p. 57.

God who accomplished everything, that he was only God's humble servant; that God had chosen him, a man of patience, fidelity and discipline, when the time came for Prussia, German unity, and European peace."

European peace! It rests—at least so the story goes—in the red portfolio of one who hardly invokes the grace of God and who no more sees himself as the instrument of Providence than he does as the instrument of his sovereign. It rests on one whose declared motto, a motto which is indeed the last that the master he was called upon to serve would have chosen, is: "The great illness of this century is the fear of responsibility."

The Chancellor does not come every day to the Palace. When the business at hand is not or *ought not* to be important, his son Herbert calls on the Emperor. Count Herbert affects the mannerisms of his father, imitates his handwriting and sees himself already clearly as the next chancellor, if not as the Crown Prince himself, as John Lemoine once called him in the *Journal des Débats*.

Last summer, at the time of the Alexander of Bulgaria affair,[5] the Chancellor left Berlin

[5] Prince Alexander ("Sandro") of Battenberg had been appointed ruler of the newly created kingdom of Bulgaria,

every afternoon and came to Babelsberg to con-
fer with the Emperor.

The Chancellor always arrives in a closed carriage; he never shows himself to Berliners either
in an open carriage or on foot, but only in uniform on horseback, on the bridlepaths, and he is
never seen at court receptions or entertainments.
The Chancellor is buttoned up tight in his yellow cuirassier uniform; he leaves his cap in his
carriage and dons his formidable polished metal
helmet. He enters, crosses the vestibule, head
held high, like a master, his red portfolio under
his arm. He doesn't have to give himself airs,
for nature has served him monstrously well in
that respect, and one can understand that such a
giant figure, tightly buttoned up in such a bar-
barous uniform, graced with such terrifying

---

and when Princess Victoria (1866–1929), the daughter of
the Crown Prince, known as "Moretta," fell in love with
him, she split the German court in two because Bulgaria
was in the sphere of influence of Germany's ally, Russia. All
this led to a contest between the Crown Princess and Bismarck, who opposed the marriage of Moretta and Sandro
and won hands down. Moretta later married another German prince who was killed in World War I. At the age of
sixty-one, still incurably romantic, she married a Russian
adventurer half her age, riding pillion on his motorcycle
and proposing to fly the Atlantic with him, until he left her
to die penniless. See below, p. 119 and *The Kaisers*, pp.
123–31 and 179–83.

white eyebrows, and an old lion's face, can allow himself a few "responsibilities."

Sometimes the Chancellor waits in the ante-chamber, and he is then most curious to watch. He has positively the appearance of a wild-man; he madly scrutinizes the most insignificant knickknacks, stops suddenly, scratches his cheek as he does in the Reichstag when he is about to speak, and looks at you without seeing you. The Chancellor enters the Emperor's study; the tête-à-tête begins. All one can say is that if the Chancellor is master, he shows himself with regard to his sovereign as extremely humble, imbued with veneration, and calls him in private as in public "Master" and swears that he is "his old servant." One could not be more realistic.

It is in his study that the Emperor receives, it is there that he lives, in this tiny corner of this tiny palace. The Emperor inhabits the left corner of the ground floor, and the Empress the corresponding corner of the floor above. No luxury or comfort in this palace: not a sign of a bathroom, for instance. The whole place is furnished with an odd assortment of Christmas

presents, gifts from China and Japan, offerings
from diverse national delegations on the occasion of various anniversaries and purchases
made in Paris at the Exposition of 1867. The
tradition of thrift among the Hohenzollerns is
well-known: once it was because of poverty, but
no longer. When he came to the throne, William I had nothing but debts: the Civil List of
the King of Prussia is nine million francs. None
has been established for the Emperor of Germany. Today William I is rich: only one man,
the banker Kohn, knows the exact size of his fortune. One would not be far wrong in putting his
personal income at eighteen million francs. The
Emperor wishes to be kept informed of the
slightest expenditure. The Palace personnel are
extremely limited and composed of not very de-
manding veterans. The highest salary of the
court entourage is some thirty thousand francs.[6]
The administrators are consequently on the
alert: they have a special aversion for a trio of
French chefs imposed by the good taste of the
Empress, who are thought to be making a for-

[6] This was the salary of Count Perponcher, the Court Chamberlain. Laforgue's salary as Reader to the Empress Augusta
was nine thousand francs. An American dollar at the time
was equal to five French francs.

tune with aristocratic abandon. Examples of the meanness abound: if given in detail, they would appear grotesquely improbable.

The Sovereign's study is filled with military and family souvenirs. On the table is a bouquet of cornflowers that is constantly refreshed; in one corner, some flags. In Berlin the Emperor never takes off his general's uniform, old and somewhat worn as it is. At his window he appears in it with the Pour le Mérite Cross around his neck every day at noon when the guard passes, led by the band. In the evening a curtain is pulled down across this window, through which is still visible the bowed head of the Emperor working by the light of a simple lamp; the maudlin crowds gather to observe this spectacle under the eyes of the policemen who guard the palace.

Only the Emperor and the Empress with her personal attendants[7] are lodged in the Palace. The Emperor is in his study, going over old papers, the Empress is upstairs with her ladies. The Palace is quiet as if uninhabited, especially in the afternoon and evening.

In the morning the ground floor is somewhat

[7]There were four: two women of the wardrobe and two women of the bedchamber.

enlivened by voices and by the clanking of spurs.

After one o'clock in the afternoon everything lapses again into silence. The valets play cards, leaf through old magazines, yawn, at times even desert the vestibule: there are indeed moments when anyone could enter the Palace just as one would enter a mill.

The Emperor and the Empress live as separately as possible in Berlin, and in the summer, they manage not to be together. They dine separately, take separate walks, never appear together in public. In the evening, around eleven o'clock, when the Empress, in the care of her ladies-in-waiting, reads *Le Figaro*, the Emperor comes up for a moment. These ladies-in-waiting are old friends of the Emperor's, who wear as charms the bits of lead extracted from his wound after the attempt on his life in 1878.[8]

[8]"On the afternoon of Sunday, 2 June 1878, as the Kaiser's calèche went bowling along Unter den Linden towards the Brandenburg Gate, a sudden sound of gunfire shattered the summer air. A shotgun had been fired at the carriage from a second floor window of No. 18. The Emperor, in the act of waving acknowledgement to the cheers of the Sunday afternoon strollers, was peppered with shot. He was hit in the back, the neck and the right arm, with some of the shot ripping through his helmet and grazing his forehead. Streaming blood, he was driven back to his palace at breakneck

One of them, the oldest, was the only person, together with a matron of honor, to accompany him on his flight in 1848. The Sovereign chats intimately for a moment about the evening at the Opera, about his audiences that day, and about what has been said at tea. His good humor is unfailing, it would seem, and always gives way gently before the unfailing ill humor of the Empress, just as he formerly gave way before her great fits of temper, merely murmuring under his breath: "It's nothing, just her Russian blood that comes from her grandfather Tsar Paul of Russia."

In the morning the Empress, at about ten o'clock, comes down to visit the Emperor. This is usually the only time when Their Majesties speak to each other in private. Politics can scarcely be said to be the chief subject of their

---

speed and carried up to his rooms. Over thirty grains of shot were removed from his body. Throughout the incident the eighty-one-year-old Emperor remained remarkably composed but the loss of blood had considerably weakened him and it was doubted that he would last the night. . . . The would-be assassin was a Dr. Karl Nobiling. A well-educated member of a wealthy middle-class family, Nobiling seems to have had no political connections. . . . [he] died of self-inflicted wounds before he could be properly questioned." *The Kaisers*, p. 110.

conversation. The Empress, who has given up interfering in state business, especially religious business, and has given it up to such an extent that she is even reconciled with her old enemy Prince Bismarck, the Empress today is satisfied, like any private person, to be kept informed by Wolff's telegrams and the résumés in the *Temps* and *Débats* (the latter two, it seems, explain what is happening in Germany better than the *Cologne Gazette*). It is rather of a certain marriage in, or close to, the family that they converse, of a certain approaching, quite delicate, audience, and of the next ball. It is of the peculiar state of affairs existing between the two sovereigns and the house of the Crown Prince, and of the attitude to be taken in that respect today or tomorrow, even concerning the slightest detail.

This is, in fact, the chief subject of conversation in both palaces. More and more, one feels that the hour will sound when one side will replace the other. The Emperor knows that his best servants may well fall out of favor and that his work may be ruined. The Empress feels that, as a widow, her life in Berlin and even in Germany will be made impossible by the new sovereign, that foreigner with overly modern taste, whose influence has already robbed her of the affection and respect of her son; and she has talked for a long time of retiring to Rome.

In the palace of the Crown Prince the exasperation increases daily. The Prince grows old with inaction: his father is too jealous of his power to give him the slightest hand in military or civil affairs. But the causes of the discord are complex. The authority of the head of the family is with the Hohenzollerns a sacred principle that can be carried to extremes. Even at fifty, the present sovereign was only Crown Prince and had to yield, with his wife the Crown Princess, to the whims and often senile demands of the king, and this king was only his brother. In turn, the Emperor and the Empress today use their power over the Heir-Apparent, and especially over his wife, the Crown Princess, with a severity that is at times incredible. The Prince cannot take a step nor spend a cent without consulting his father and he is made to feel this dependence quite strongly.

The Crown Princess cannot choose a lady-in-waiting for herself nor a governess for the princesses, her daughters, cannot travel, cannot allow herself to be accompanied on a journey by such and such a lady, nor permit her daughters to take part in an entertainment or charity bazaar, without the consent of her haughty and often sharp-tongued mother-in-law.

On the other hand, the Crown Prince is not on good terms with his son Prince William, who has achieved popularity in the army by making a show of his worship of the Emperor. That is enough to have made the two sovereigns openly spoil their grandson and his house. The result of all this is a series of pin-pricks and snubs flaunted even publicly at court balls, and it is easy to guess how all this will end.

Already a few clever people are scheming to be on the right side of the broom when it sweeps clean. And yet, after all, this famous cleaning day may well be quite harmless: the ever-changing nature of the future sovereign has until now allowed nothing but guesses with respect to external or internal affairs as well as court life. Only painters can be sure that for them this change of reign will mean a change of artistic reign as well, the need for which is more than slightly felt in Berlin.

What is the Emperor's nature? When this question is put to one of the court insiders, especially a woman, the reply is almost always the same:

the Emperor is *goldig*, he is *golden*. And that, in fact, is the word that occurs to you, a foreigner, at the very sound of the Sovereign's voice, before his affable and noble manners, before his honest and open actions so frequently mentioned.

But this is only, if one may say so, the Monarch's "secondary manner." Those insiders who have lived for fifty years at the court have known a very different "first manner." The prince, dignified, correct, detesting familiarities, not limiting to the army his respect if not his interest, a willing listener, not opinionated on any subject, avoiding what might be taken for historical utterances, the Sovereign whom we see today was fashioned first by the Empress Augusta, a superior woman who lived up in every way to the ideal she had formed of her rank, and then by the providential, and, to him sacred, aspect of the sudden events of which he found himself, late in his life, the unconscious instrument.

The Crown Prince of earlier years, with his advantages as a handsome soldier, with his mental powers that confined him to the pure practical study of the army, seemed to have no other aim than to win the nickname that was openly given him of *unteroffizier—non-commissioned officer*, to be a true Prussian non-commissioned officer, proud of his moustache, a breaker of hearts, scorning the university, books, music, fine arts, everything except his uniform and the parade, and, withal, laying down the law on every subject. Princess Augusta, of Russian origin, brought up at Weimar, in the company of Goethe, reared in the admiration of the great French century and who, even today, at seventy-six, reviews nearly every morning her collection of elegant French expressions, the Princess compelled the non-commissioned officer to take with her, three times a week, a course in litera-ture which a professor came to give them at the palace; she made him stimulate his conversa-tion, reform his manners, and be sparing with his handshakes.

The non-commissioned officer was born good and gentle; he did what he could. He had married for reasons of state: the Empress quickly gave him his liberty, but retained her influence. The Emperor has always kept for the Empress the humblest respect: the Empress has always remained for him a special being, of another race, whose superior nervous make-up would not admit of any interference, and even her anti-Germanic tastes and manners must be respected.

Not only in Paris, which is far away, does the Sovereign's health cause false alarms. Every winter in Berlin there comes a time when at the slightest rumor of his illness suddenly the shops selling mourning apparel are besieged. The Emperor rarely passes a week without fainting from weakness, and sometimes that happens several days in succession. It's the end, people think. The next day nothing happens: on the contrary, the Sovereign receives his visitors, appears to his public. And it has been thus for six years without any visible change. One of the court doctors told me: "He is the picture of perfect health until the first strong wind blows."

5

THE EMPRESS

While the Emperor is, by nature, simple and self-effacing, the Empress[1] is complicated and makes her presence felt.

The Empress is a descendant of Catherine the Great of Russia, she was brought up at Weimar, she has constantly lived in admiration of the ancient French court, French salons, the French language. She married the Crown Prince of Prussia for state reasons. The good, kindly Prince left behind him a doomed passion for a Princess Radziwill, who is now dead.[2] Proud

[1] Maria Luisa Augusta Catherina of Saxe-Weimar (1811–90) was seventy-six years old when Laforgue composed the present portrait.

[2] Princess Elisa Radziwill, with whom William I fell in love at the age of twenty-four. As the second son of the King of Prussia, William was expected to marry a princess of royal

Empress Augusta.
Schloss Charlottenburg Mausoleum, Berlin.

and alien to any sort of sentimentality, Princess Augusta saw in this union only her elevation to a rank to which she was uniquely destined by birth and for which she felt, to be precise, an artistic vocation. Cut out to be neither wife nor mother nor grandmother, as they say of her at court, she resumed her freedom as soon as she had produced an heir to the throne. From then on, she gave herself up completely to this role of queen, of which her ideal conception was as nobly bare as it was unusually imposing. She has come to constitute a strange character, artificial but logical and fascinating, who has charmed all the ambassadors to Berlin as well as all cultivated visitors, including M. de Lesseps himself.[3]

Concerning M. de Lesseps, I might say it would not surprise me if the idea of his Berlin visit had not been first discreetly put to him by the Empress herself. At the Empress's daily

---

blood. He was forced to renounce Elisa Radziwill, who, although well born, was not of a reigning house. She died brokenhearted not long afterwards.

[3] Ferdinand Marie, Vicomte de Lesseps (1805–94), French diplomat who planned and supervised the construction of the Suez Canal (1859–69). In his "Chronique parisienne," published in April 1887, detailing the events of March of that year, Laforgue also refers to Ferdinand de Lesseps' journey to Berlin.

teas, every time anyone alluded to the "great Frenchman"—and he was the favorite subject of conversation of her friend, the Duke of Sagan, who steers the conversation at the Empress's table—every time the same conclusion was reached: "To think that I might have made his acquaintance at the time of the Exposition! A misunderstanding prevented me from doing so. I also had the chance to see M. Michel Chevalier and all those gentlemen (the Saint-Simonians),[4] but M. de Lesseps was not there. Alas! Will I never see him?" A slight pretext presented itself, a decoration conferred on our ambassador, M. Herbette; the insignia could be brought by his old friend M. de Lesseps, who had nothing else to do at the moment. The Duke of Sagan immediately took advantage of the occasion and arranged the whole affair. So you see what diplomatic feats our charming compatriot has come out of retirement to perform.

In looks and bearing, as in character, the Empress has nothing German about her. To judge from her portraits, even the one by Win-

[4]The followers of Claude Henri de Rouvroy, Comte de Saint-Simon (1760–1825), who called for abolition of inheritance rights, public control of means of production, and the gradual emancipation of women.

terhalter, who also painted the Empress Eugénie and knew his job, the Empress Augusta has never been what one would call beautiful. Everything about her is a little masculine, her extreme height, her voice, her hands. Her complexion, which is naturally swarthy, is quite clearly covered by make-up to which only a Berlin woman could object: it goes so well with all this deliberate dress, these youthful, flowery prints that look as if they were meant to adorn an idol, with these affected manners, with this voice which, while basically harsh, is maintained on a shrill, fragile, and doleful key.

The first word uttered by this mournful and rather sibylline voice is always to say how exhausted, half-dead the lady is, while across her forehead she slowly passes a long pale hand, with a single ring on her ring finger, an extraordinarily well-cared-for hand, of which she is quite proud. One has before one a being all nerves, who seems only to endure because of them, an emaciated, worn face with eyes of an imperceptible but implacable gray. These terrible eyes are known for nailing people down and many a lady-in-waiting has had her difficulties getting accustomed to them. But as soon as the mouth smiles, especially since the smile always looks rather forced, one has the feeling of receiving an unmerited favor, and our august town council itself, hardened as it is, could not resist it. The Empress lives on nothing: tea, two fingers of champagne, and other such things. Since the age of nine, she has not passed a day without taking some sort of medicine; at seventy, almost at death's door, she underwent one of the most delicate operations; a fall which she suffered five years ago was poorly treated, and has left her condemned to a wheelchair. By dint of her energy, she has succeeded in getting up, taking several steps, and gives the illusion at times that she can receive standing up. And moreover, her mind is still lively, her memory surprising; her eye sees everything and takes everything in, her ear catches the slightest whisper in a general conversation.

The Empress is Protestant, of course, but there has been a great Catholic influence in her life. Catholicism, in its political and social spirit, as well as in its moral code, particularities of form, and resources for the soul, has constantly been, alas, her almost Platonic preoccupation. It has also something of the aspect of forbidden fruit. It is said that were she a widow, the Sovereign would go live in Rome and very probably would be converted there. Four years ago, when Germany was celebrating the fourth centenary of Luther[5] and the whole court was officially in Berlin, the Empress remained quietly ensconced in her castle at Coblenz. The Sovereign loves to surround herself with Catholics; the title of Catholic is for her a recommendation. Needless to say, it is abused. For example, letters are received quite often from French priests, evidently not in good standing, asking for monetary assistance. But the lady of the Palace in general charge of "external affairs,"[6] whose duty it is to open and reply to these letters, is a diplomat worthy of being a cashier, and does not easily let money slip from her mistress's cashbox.

This Catholic influence has come to the Empress, like much that makes up her life, from France, from a Frenchman. This man, who died before the war, was the secretary to whom Talleyrand dictated his *Mémoires*; he is none other than the great-uncle of the author of *Au-*

[5] On November 10, 1883.
[6] Countess von Hacke.

tour d'un Mariage.[7] He was French consul at Karlsruhe and lived much of the time at Baden-Baden. A sort of mystic friendship was established between the Queen of Prussia and this personage who seemed to one or two court skeptics a charming Jesuit, while to the Empress's whole entourage, he was a model of refinement and knowledge. His photograph is displayed on a number of tables at the Palace, and the anniversary of his death is observed with mute sadness. "How fortunate that he died before this war!" the Empress still exclaims.

For the Emperor, all this goes with his wife's intellectual activities, her superior make-up: it has nothing to do with him.

Berliners believe that the Empress is swallowed up in exercises of piety. This is certainly not the case. The Empress does not have the temperament of a religious bigot, nor has she taken on the habits, language or look of one. Al-

[7]Adolphe Fourier de Bacourt (1801–65), who was the great-uncle of "Gyp" (1849–1932), alias the Comtesse Sibylle de Martel de Janville. Gyp's book, to which Laforgue refers, was actually *Autour du mariage.* The day of Bacourt's death, remembered in sad silence, was 4 April. Gyp sometimes visited the Empress (see *Looking for Laforgue,* pp. 66–67).

though all her sympathies and convictions as both woman and sovereign lean toward Catholicism, her upbringing was quite Protestant. And even in the atmosphere of Rome, she would not follow in the footsteps of Madame Gervaisais,[8] whose story has held her interest so completely, without in any way upsetting her.

Convinced of her superiority and domineering by nature—all the more domineering because of the Emperor's predilection for submitting to political tutelage—the Empress was bound to be attracted to dabbling in matters of state. Herr von Bismarck always quietly put a stop to this. At the time of the religious affairs of the *Kulturkampf*,[9] which the Empress took particularly to

[8] In the novel of the same name by Edmond and Jules de Goncourt.

[9] "The *Kulturkampf* was Germany's version of that general nineteenth-century problem—the conflict between the State and the Roman Catholic Church. To liberals this *Kulturkampf* was looked upon as a war between enlightenment and obscurantism; to Catholics it was a defence of the rights of the Church; to Bismarck it was an opportunity to break the Church's power. As it was the National Liberal Party in the Reichstag that opposed the Church and the newly-formed Centre Party that defended it, Bismarck was forced into a somewhat uncomfortable alliance with the National Liber-

heart, the struggle was lively and the two sides
were found to be irreconcilable. The Chancellor
knew that, as always, with everyone, he would
have the last word. He played his hand by remaining calm and waiting for the disfavor to
end of its own accord, and for the Sovereign to
give him her hand again to kiss on New Year's
day. As on many other occasions, he could not
forego his favorite pleasure, the use of swear
words. His exact words naturally only traveled
on the level of gossip, but the Empress's Chamberlain received one full in the face before
everyone. One day when Herr von Bismarck
came as usual to see the Emperor, her Chamberlain, who happened to be there in the antechamber where the court officers come and go, turned
his back on him and began to drum with his fin-
gertips on a windowpane. And the Chancellor
said in a loud voice for all to hear: "Who wants
to set foot in a house when you can't even get the
flunkeys to greet you?"

Today they are again on good terms; the rec-

---

als. With their support, he passed a series of harsh laws
against the clergy. In this long struggle, he came up against
the implacable opposition of the Empress." *The Kaisers*,
p. 100.

onciliation took place four years ago. The extent of the Chancellor's bowing and scraping, and the veneration he puts in his voice are surprising even to the entourage of the Empress. *Commediante, tragediante*! one may say of him as the Pope said of Napoleon.

Berliners never have a chance to see their Sovereign, do not know her, are not interested in what she does and certainly would be incapable of saying whether or not she is in Berlin, has just left or is going to return. The Empress never appears with the Emperor, and never goes out in an open carriage. The photographs seen of her in the shopwindows of Berlin are copied from busts, medallions, drawings entirely composed and corrected under her personal supervision, according to her specifications.

The Empress is unpopular in Berlin. It is not so much because of her French sympathies; they are not generally known, and besides are a matter about which Germans are less sensitive than we would be under the circumstances. No, but the Empress never appears and seems consequently to disdain her place at the Emperor's side. She is said to be Catholic and devout, she is hostile to the Chancellor, she is a stickler for protocol, she dislikes beer, she hates all the sweet and simple things dear to the German heart, she is incapable of *Gemüt*; she is, in short, not "from these parts."

Are they better known in France, these French sympathies of hers, which, while remaining within tactful limits, are nothing short of platonic? In one of M. Rothan's[10] books one reads this note: "The name of the Empress Augusta should only be pronounced with respect in France." His note is accompanied by facts to justify it; one could easily supply others. When you tour the valley of the Rhine, stop at Coblenz and visit the charming cemetery for French soldiers who died during their internment; the Empress is wholly responsible for this cemetery, and she alone pays for its upkeep.

The Empress speaks French perfectly, and with no accent whatever. But a peculiar thing about her French is that when she is in an agreeable frame of mind, it tends, through the preciosity of carefully chosen expressions and the childish and somewhat ironic affectation of its

[10]Gustave Rothan, author of *The Origins of the War of 1870*, published in 1879, and of several volumes of diplomatic memoirs, two of which had appeared in 1882 and 1884.

slow intonations, to constitute a kind of wit that one follows with pleasure. Only at first, when one is still poorly oriented to this sovereign presence, in which everything seems designed to put one off, does it seem really affected.

While partaking of her only real pleasure, tea-time conversation, the Empress delights in replying with a quip in French; it is the sort of quip that is impossible in German, but when used in a French comedy, is sure to charm a foreign audience. Although it goes without saying that these retorts, especially in a conversation in France, would almost never be called for, yet the Empress forces the occasion and meets it, and that's that. One afternoon at tea, telling of some unusual happening, the Empress added: "In short, it made my hair stand on end." The Chamberlain, a plump harmless character, began to laugh agreeably. And the Empress, seizing the occasion, cut him with a glance, whipping out so quickly that no one understood and the whole pleasure was for herself alone: "I must say that that's the last thing that could happen to me," alluding to what one can only guess.[11]

Love of the French language could not be car-

---

[11] Laforgue had noted this quip in his *Agenda* for 1883 on 3 May, when the Empress had undoubtedly made it.

ried farther than it is by the Empress, who imposes it like another sovereign presence and insists on using it on every possible occasion, and often insists too vehemently. The Empress and her daughter[12]—the latter is nothing but a German imitation of her mother—always write to each other in French; when visiting an exhibition in Dresden, I believe it was, they could even be heard chatting in French as they moved through the crowd.

The Empress received, as was the custom in her youth, all the education needed to preside over a Dresden tea service. The Empress still reads a great deal, and what she reads is, needless to say, French. Every morning, the *Figaro*, the *Temps*, and the *Débats* are placed on her table, and every fortnight, the head valet, a Frenchman,[13] is given the *Revue des deux mondes* so he may cut the pages. She is especially fond of memoirs and reminiscences. From time to time a novel: Octave Feuillet is always welcome and remains the first of the few who may be read in

[12] Luisa, the daughter of William and Augusta, married the Grand Duke of Baden.
[13] Francis Corbeil, valet of Empress Augusta 1858–90. See *Looking for Laforgue*, pp. 72–74.

their entirety. Pierre Loti is delightful in extracts. It is also by means of extracts that she fulfills her obligations to the "new school," that is, the Goncourts, Zola, Daudet, whose language is a bit too revolutionary for a faithful reader of the *Revue des deux mondes*. There is one writer of whom she reads every word: Maxime du Camp,[14] an old friend who returns every summer to Baden-Baden. What happy evenings she owes to this old skeptic's presence at Parisian charity balls! There is another writer, and only one, who is systematically excluded from the Empress's library, and that is Renan, naturally because of his *Life of Jesus*.

Like a proper eighteenth-century woman, the Empress is interested only in genre painting and in Italian music, or music of an even lighter nature. When she is forced to accompany some royal guest to the Opera and sit through two acts of Wagner, it is more than her delicate nerves can stand.

In any event, the Empress no longer goes to the Opera since she suffered her fall. Five years

---

[14] Maxime du Camp (1822–94), travel writer and man of letters. A friend of Flaubert, whom he accompanied to the East, he died at Baden-Baden.

ago, however, every time the Berlin Opera gave *Carmen*, which was once a week, the people of Berlin knew where they could be sure of setting eyes on their invisible sovereign. Still today, at noon, when the Guardsmen march by the Palace with the band in the lead, if the bandleader wants to be agreeable, he can do nothing better than play a march from Bizet's opera. During the winter, the Empress gives what are known as her "Musical Thursdays." These are mainly occasions for receiving the diplomatic corps and for organizing a little French conversation. A majority of the great virtuosi have played on these occasions. Sarasate is still the spoiled child and Rubinstein is kept away only because of his unsociability.

The Empress lives in Berlin from the first of December to the first of May. She divides her time between the Augusta Hospital and the Augusta Boarding School. When one sees a carriage, a heavy brougham with a body low enough to receive the Empress's wheelchair, leaving the Palace as usual by a rear gate, one can be sure that she is on the way to one or the other of her places of refuge. To them goes also the greater part of her money. The Red Cross and the German Health societies are also regular occupations for which she employs a secretary.

After the first of May begins a series of stops in Baden-Baden, Coblenz, and Homburg, where the Empress and her household, reduced to a minimum, live quite informally either in the local castle when there is one, or in a hotel. The Chamberlain and the ladies-in-waiting are changed every month. The Chamberlain is usually a country squire, a baron or a count, who doesn't know what to do with his hands when he has put down his teacup. The ladies-in-waiting are young countesses who are made to come for a month from their castles, and who only know how to say, "Yes, Your Majesty! No, Your Majesty!" and who are afterwards sent back with a small gift.

At Baden-Baden the Empress has the great distraction of visits from her daughter and from the Grand Duke, and almost daily visits with the Duchess Hamilton and her inseparable lady friend, the Countess Tascher de la Pagerie,[15]

[15]Stéphanie, Comtesse Tascher de la Pagerie (1814–1905), a personage of the court of Napoleon III, published her memoirs in 1893–95.

who may leave behind some rather spirited memoirs.

In Berlin the Empress's household consists of a Grand Mistress and two ladies-in-waiting; one of them lives with the memory of her great beauty and past royal favors, the other is the Empress's strong right arm.[16] In addition, there is a permanent lady-in-waiting, a chamberlain, a doctor, a secretary and four Women of the Bedchamber, of whom the first is the one person out of the entire court capable of writing the most curious and complete memoirs, which she will never do. We might add that all this society has not been very closely observed by the author of *Berlin Society*.[17]

---

[16] The Grand Mistress of the Household was Countess Perponcher and the two palace ladies (*palast damen*) were Countess von Oriola and Countess von Hacke. Countess von Oriola lived on memories of her great beauty and Countess von Hacke was the Empress's strong right arm. The chief personal attendant was Marianne von Neindorf, first Woman of the Bedchamber, who, as Laforgue predicted, did not leave any memoirs.

[17] *La Société à Berlin* by Catherine Radziwill, published in Paris in 1883 under the pseudonym of "Count Paul Vasili." It was thought in Berlin at the time that the greater part of it was the work of the first Reader to the Empress, Auguste Gérard, journalist and later diplomat. He was dismissed from his post, and the book was banned in Berlin. See Appendix to *Berlin, la cour et la ville*.

The one feature lacking in this portrait of the Empress is perhaps easy to guess. The Empress is a superior person; she is certainly of a race infinitely superior to her surroundings. She feels it, she reads it in the eyes of all about her; all is adoration around her and there is no one in her entourage who has not had to endure the cruelties of her pride and the caprices of her great boredom. The Empress has spent her life not being able to adjust to her milieu, dreaming of a Catholic monarchy and French salons. She has been bored, she is still bored, and she still dreams.

Her greatest distraction is the arrival of some foreign guest whom she must receive. The waiting is feverish; after the departure there is a period of letdown and most often of harsh words. Let us hope that M. de Lesseps will have lived up to expectations and have proved neither overly flattering nor overly pedantic, nor too technical in the explanation of the plans of his canal.

I have spoken of the extraordinary vitality of the Empress in the apparent ruin of her health. If, as they say, the Emperor is made of gold, then the Empress is made of steel. Once a widow, she will undoubtedly retire to Rome:

only there, whether she is converted or not, may she find at last consolation and advice on her withdrawal. There she will, at least, have the sun, the good sun she loves so much.[18]

[18] Laforgue was wrong; Augusta did not retire to Rome after the death of William I in 1889. She threw herself into court life with renewed vigor on the accession of her grandson, William II, seeming to sacrifice her liberal principles for a taste of pomp and power. See *The Kaisers*, pp. 215–16.

6

THE COURT BALL

Their Majesties give four balls each winter. The series opens with a reception in which a concert takes the place of a ball, and closes on the twenty-second of March, on the Emperor's birthday, with an evening devoted to opera and ballet. The first and last parties are more intimate and less crowded than the balls. At these four balls all Berlin may be seen, especially military Berlin, although almost none of artistic Berlin, of which the Emperor never invites more than the official flower, leaving the remainder for the receptions of the Crown Prince and Crown Princess, who patronize the arts.

One fine morning a messenger brings you your invitation, a card wrapped with a folded program. The card bears the words:

By order of Their Imperial and Royal
Majesties, the undersigned Court Marshal has
the honor to invite Mr. . . . to the ball and to
the supper of . . . at half past eight, at the
*Royal Palace (*Königliches Schloss*).*

    Signed:

      Count PERPONCHER

This invitation, surmounted by the imperial crown, is decorated by an ornamented border displaying the arms of the two Majesties and a view of the Royal Palace, the whole thing framed by laurel and ivy, and rather poorly executed.

The first leaf of the program that wraps the invitation card says that the ball will take place in the White Hall (*Weisse Saal*) of the Royal Palace (this room is reserved exclusively for receptions, which means that one is rather cramped for space at parties given by the Crown Prince in this same Palace) that the ladies will appear in evening dress (décolleté), the men in full dress, the army in full dress uniform for state occasions (this uniform has nothing particular about it except the white duck trousers), that Their Highnesses will arrive at 9:00 P.M., will enter by the steps of the Knights' Hall and meet in the Black

Eagle Room (*Schwarze Adler Kammer*), that the diplomatic corps will assemble in the White Hall, generals, high functionaries, and others will arrive at a quarter past eight and will assemble in the Chapel Room (*Kapitelsaal*), and finally that the other guests will arrive at 8:30 P.M. in the Picture Gallery. The second sheet of the program designates in much the same way, according to protocol, the entry to the refreshment tables.

From eight o'clock on, Unter den Linden, almost empty and usually very quiet at this hour between the Imperial Palace and the Royal Palace, is filled by the monotonous and continuous noise of the carriages. The state carriages arrive only at the last moment; the poor cabs open the march. If it is not raining, most of the soldiers come on foot, stiff in their trousers with foot straps, correct in their black greatcoats, some wearing simply a little cap, while behind them, orderlies carry their helmets in boxes. All along Unter den Linden mounted policemen keep order with implacable zeal. The avenue already seems like an antechamber of the Royal Palace. The environs of the Royal Palace are ruthlessly cleared of every pedestrian who has no invitation: the crowd has the right to assemble only on the opposite sidewalk, from which it may contemplate the passing carriages without even seeing the fortunate guests dismount from them. And yet the people remain there nevertheless until midnight, often with their feet in the snow, gaping at the lighted windows. The good Berliner never tires of admiring court carriages. On every occasion on which these vehicles, almost worthy of a Musée de Cluny, are made to take the air, he waits between the two palaces to see them shuttle back and forth, adorned by powdered coachmen in three-cornered tasseled hats and their pairs of lackeys in silver livery, pink silk stockings and two-cornered plumed hats, carrying maces or swords.

The Imperial Palace, inhabited by Their Majesties, is just big enough for the Empress's intimate receptions and Musical Thursdays. Court Balls are held in the Royal Palace at the end of Unter den Linden, across from the museums, five minutes from the other palaces, ten minutes from the embassies.

The Royal Palace is a building quite simple in appearance, built in a light eighteenth-century style, white-washed here and there, surrounding, with a height of four storeys (forming about six hundred rooms), two courtyards and a chapel with a cupola. The courtyards have retained the rough paving stones of the days when heavy carriages had triple-ironed wheels.

The Picture Gallery is the rendezvous assigned to ordinary guests. But apart from these guests, deputies, professors, artists, rank-and-file officers, numerous others and in general all those who like their comfort and do not have to conform to the program have taken the habit of assembling in this room. This gallery, which is quite long, has interesting pictures and corners where one can sit and chat while drinking tea. Moreover, it has the advantage of coming immediately before the White Hall, which means that by taking a good seat, one can watch the guests go by—the diplomatic corps first, and then the court.

From nine o'clock on, the Picture Gallery presents a double row fifty meters long, bedecked with civilian and military uniforms, in which a black dress coat is rare and a chest free of decorations absolutely not to be found.

Just think of the fact that Germany with all her small states has at least one hundred decorations listed in her Military Yearbook, begin-

ning with the four varieties of the Order of the
Red Eagle! But let us examine the pictures.

The immense chromo of Anton von Werner,[1]
"The Proclamation of the Empire at Versailles,"
with the helmets of the cuirassier guards mi-
nutely reflecting the windows of the palace;
"The Coronation of King William I at Konigs-
berg" by Menzel,[2] an interesting essay in real-
ism and even impressionism in an official picture; a Prince of Wales in a Prussian hussar's
uniform; some genre paintings concerned with
the last war; and a number of old paintings by
the Frenchman Pesne.[3] "Bonaparte Crossing

[1] Anton Alexander von Werner (1843–1915) had accompanied the Crown Prince in the Franco-Prussian War. Director of the Berlin Academy (1875–1915), he produced popular paintings illustrating Prussian history.

[2] Adolph von Menzel (1815–1905), self-taught painter of
the German Realist School. A small man, almost a dwarf, he
became a professor decorated with the Order of the Black
Eagle. His paintings in the 1840s and 1850s anticipated the
Impressionists; but when shown the works of the Impressionists, including a Monet, a Degas, and a Manet, being
exhibited in Berlin, works which inspired Laforgue to write
his essay on Impressionism, he asked their owner, "Have
you really paid money for this trash?" See *Imperial Berlin*,
pp. 222–23.

[3] Antoine Pesne (1683–1757) was appointed Prussian court
painter in 1711. While Crown Prince, Frederick the Great
became his patron. Pesne produced frescoes and murals as
well as easel paintings in Berlin and Potsdam.

the Alps" by David used to be here, but it has
been gone for the past two years.

We point out the celebrities to one another:
the Rector of the University, in a red velvet coat
embroidered with gold and pumps with buck-
les; the illustrious Mommsen,[4] who is not well
thought of at court, with his look of an old
sorcerer and his nervous gestures, who speaks
French in a charming way and enjoys speaking
ill of Duruy;[5] the scholar Helmholtz,[6] who had
himself knighted to please his wife—by marry-
ing she had lost the *von* from her name; the violinist Joachim;[7] the painter Menzel, no taller
than a cuirassier-guard's boot, bedecked with
pendants and orders, but also wearing the Le-
gion of Honor, coming and going, knowing
everyone, not missing a single one of these par-

[4]Theodor Mommsen (1817–1903), author of the monumental *History of Rome*, taught and wrote in Berlin from
1858 until his death. See below, p. 150.
[5]Victor Duruy (1811–94) was French minister of public education under the Second Empire.
[6]Herman Ludwig Ferdinand von Helmholtz (1821–94),
author of *Treatise on Physiological Optics* (1827), was a pio-
neer in the subject; he extended Thomas Young's theory of
color vision.
[7]Joseph Joachim (1831–1907), violinist. Director of the
Academy of Music, he introduced chamber music to
Berlin.

ties, moving among all these personages like a gnome and like the greatest *enfant terrible* for the chronicler.

Minister von Puttkamer, in his fine embroidered habit, with his eagle pendant, struts proudly about. Count Herbert von Bismarck appears now and then, twisting his thick moustache, fumbling with his monocle under this Jovian eyebrows, coldly cracking his coarse jokes. And everywhere there are officers saluting, snapping in two and replacing their monocles, everywhere chamberlains striped with gold, their ceremonial canes in their hands, their golden keys on their backs, hanging from bows of blue silk.

Then, one by one, the Embassy staffs file by, grouped behind their respective ambassadors, gazing straight ahead, knowing almost no one. They are the ones who cause the most excitement in the double rows, especially among the new guests. The French Embassy staff goes by with a willfully unobstrusive air about it, the two military attachés—two artillery officers—their undress képi in their hands, the youngest of the two, a captain, whose chest, unblemished by decorations, dumbfounds the German officers. The elder of the two attachés has been in Berlin for some time and seems quite blasé; the younger who has occupied his post for only a year has cut a very sad figure in the first balls, knowing no one and being visibly a little angry at having to file past two ranks of Prussian officers displaying their haughtiness, in spite of themselves, between two rows of paintings detailing so openly such terrible memories.

Then come the Austrian ambassador in a coat of overly perfumed fur, with his cap of heron plumes and his little tasseled boots; the Russian ambassador with his white astrakhan toque and simple soldier boots; the grave Turkish ambassador caressing his beard, the most gilded of all and the one who kisses the Empress's hand with the greatest flourish.

When the diplomatic corps has disappeared toward the White Hall, there arrives, shaking the floor with a heavy goose-step, a squad of cuirassier guards in thick white woolen uniforms, with their chests flashing, high boots and great helmets surmounted by the Prussian black spread eagle. All these guards are giants, but at times poorly formed giants, whose small pink, clean-shaven faces seem completely exhausted by an abnormal growth; with drawn sabers they take up their places two by two at the doors.

Often the cuirassier guards are replaced by old grenadier guards with moustaches and side-whiskers, wearing tall shakos and high old-fashioned gaiters.

Finally there is silence; Under-Chamberlains hurry to take their places in the ranks. At first advance with measured steps a whole hierarchy of Chamberlains in ever more glittering uniforms with canes ever more symbolically rich. Then, solitary and glowing, the Chief Marshal of the Court, Count Perponcher, very tall, his moustache waxed in the imperial manner, with the air of a Monpavon lost in some military fairyland. The Count, of Dutch origin and quite proud to hear his name given a French pronunciation, has occupied the chief position at the court for the four years that Count Pückler has been blind. Everyone at court and in Berlin pokes fun at his old-fashioned manners: he is full of his own importance, although he has a salary of only 30,000 francs to keep him going. In the long run, he is quite inoffensive.

Several steps behind him comes the Emperor, giving his arm to the Crown Princess: he, weary and stooped but still a handsome man;

she remarkable for the vivacity of her eyes that have kept their youth. All heads are lowered, but not before examining as closely as possible once again the face of the old monarch whom a puff of wind may carry off tomorrow. Afterwards comes the Crown Prince in his white cuirassier uniform, the uniform he prefers to wear, although he has the right to it only on certain occasions; he knows moreover that this slight infraction of discipline displeases his father. He seems extremely old, very worried, and no longer has the clear gaze he still possessed five years ago. He gives his arm to his daughter-in-law the Princess William, a good German girl, tall, blonde, young and smiling, untouched by court gossip.

Then comes Prince William, the next Heir-apparent. Of medium height—the stature diminishes noticeably from grandfather to grandson—he wears the most extravagant and complete red hussar uniform that can be imagined. He looks to the right and left, with a false vivacity and shakes hands all around with laughter too hearty to be true.

The Prince gives his arm to his young sister Princess Victoria, who resembles a charming

slender English girl of a particularly pleasant
and highly romantic nature. The Princess has
been thwarted in her great love for her hero
Alexander of Bulgaria.

Then there is the court beauty, Princess
Charlotte von Meiningen, the Crown Prince's
eldest daughter, married, and poorly married,
to a pauper prince, but who is, at the same time,
the subtlest and most cultivated member of the
royal family. Prince Henry, who is in the Navy,
is for the most part absent from Berlin. He is
rarely seen except at the March twenty-second
Emperor's birthday reception, the only one at
which all the young daughters of the Crown
Prince also appear.

The procession is enlarged by a group of young
German princes stationed in Berlin, among
them young Prince Leopold, son of the late
Frederick Charles. He seems not yet fully re-
covered from the terror that used to grip his wife
and children in the presence of his father. That
terrible red hussar used to frequent these balls,
always quiet, with his congested red face and
skull, ill at ease in the iron grip of his filthy
collar, adorned with chains and medals like a

Moloch.[8] Then there is Moltke[9] with his half-Danish, half-English distinction; then various aides-de-camp, the Duke of Sagan and Count Pourtalès, and then a number of generals.

Finally everyone mingles and hurries off toward the ballroom, where the orchestra has already begun the eternal "Blue Danube." The White Hall is bordered on two sides with facing rows of armchairs: one side for the court, the other for the ladies of high rank. In the back of the room, the diplomatic corps. The window bays and benches are already invaded by an odd assortment of the dancers' helmets, shakos, sabers, sabretaches, a veritable arsenal that is interesting to study. The Emperor and the Crown Prince watch the dancing for several minutes, then rise without interrupting anything. The Emperor draws together with Count Perpon-

[8]On the death of Frederick Charles (1828–85), the terrifying Red Prince, Queen Victoria wrote to her daughter "Vicky," the German Crown Princess: "There is something indescribably sad in such a death when the nearest can only be relieved by the departure of one to whom she has been bound by the nearest ties and who hated him . . . Alas! I fear his nice boy has no pleasant recollections of his poor father."
[9]General Field Marshal Helmuth Karl Bernhard Count von Moltke (1800–1891) was made Chief of the General Staff when William I became regent of Prussia in 1857.

cher and with his aide-de-camp Prince Anton Radziwill, the only man with whom he uses the familiar *du*. The Emperor will stand like this, chatting and shaking hands, for an hour, until the moment comes to retire for refreshments.

The Crown Prince stands on the other side, chatting casually with this and that guest. He no longer has the exuberant gestures and fits of laughter that he once had. The official painter Werner almost always corners him at this time, wishing to entertain him, and not realizing that he bores him to tears. Prince William also moves about, chatting, shaking hands, with his eternal false vivacity carried to an impudent extreme with the ambassadors, displaying the more than cordial manners he has learned from his father, while at the same time assuming the latter's popularity with the army. The hall gradually becomes livelier: the diplomatic corps leaves its corner and mingles, ambassadors and attachés, with the crowd. At that point, the French language takes over and bursts forth with all imaginable accents. And the awful Menzel continues to promenade.

While people are dancing and chatting in this hall, a silent and quite stylized ceremony is taking place in the Picture Gallery where we first waited. In one corner, French and English valets have withdrawn a central screen, revealing Empress Augusta enthroned on her wheelchair, raised up with cushions and draped with velvet. She is dressed quite elegantly and gotten up with every artifice, in all the Byzantine beauty of a Jezebel.

Around her, at a well-regulated distance, a circle of ladies and gentlemen, who have not yet been presented. Then the ambassadors, led by the Chamberlain Count von Nesselrode,[10] line up to kiss her hand and receive a few words, words always selected with great art and, when spoken in French, in the noblest French.

She provides a unique spectacle, this seventy-six-year-old sovereign, with no resources to fall back upon other than her nerves, her piercing glances, her fine ear, her knowing smile, her fresh memory. Now in this simple court, where the characteristics of mediocrity abound, her ideal image of a sovereign has never for a moment left her, and every day she meditates on the further nuances of it, an ideal image derived from her contemplation and study of the great French century.

[10] The Grand-Master of the Empress's household.

But it is only here, before the representatives of foreign countries, that the Empress enters with any willingness into her role and feels that something will remain of it. Germans and Berliners do not understand their Empress, who with her Russian origin has nothing German to offer the crowd, never appears in public and has done everything possible to make herself unpopular. The Empress Augusta will perhaps have been the last Empress.

An hour later, the dancing stops, the procession of Chamberlains forms again, the court follows, then, slightly behind, all the guests come streaming pell-mell. Everyone moves toward the refreshment tables set up in a dozen rooms, each destined for such and such a group, according to the program. In the opinion of foreign visitors, the buffet is tasteless in both its presentation and its offering. The good German guests enjoy it immensely and remember it with pleasure.

After the buffet, the Emperor usually retires. The procession is reformed in the direction of the White Hall where the cotillion, danced in its simplest form, is soon over.

Unter den Linden is still as neatly kept as an

antechamber, for the departure as it was for the arrival. Some military attachés permit themselves the empty pleasure of returning on foot to their embassies or their homes: only the English life-guard's tall beaver cap ever calls forth a gibe from the Berlin street urchin.

7

THE OPERA BALL

Berlin, which is still a small city with an established center and a society functioning regularly, has four balls each winter: the *Subskriptionsball*, which is the Opera Ball, at which the court appears; the *Kavaliersball*, in the halls of the Kaiserhof or the Hotel Continental, where "the most exclusive circles of the capital, the ladies and gentlemen of the highest nobility," gather twice a year; the *Presseball* in the winter garden of the Central Hotel and the *Ball der Schauspieler* ("Dramatic Artists Ball").

The Opera Ball is not a costume ball; it is a gala civilian ball given for the public and presided over by the Emperor and the court, with tickets for 10 francs. It always takes place in February —a little sooner or a little later—depending on the Emperor's health. The public includes a number of out-of-town people who have come to Berlin especially for this occasion, the only one on which the Emperor may be seen close up. If the Sovereign cannot come, according to tradition, to open the ball in person, the public, which has until the last minute hoped that he might appear, sinks into an incredible gloom.

But the old Sovereign is too imbued with his role and the thought of parades, tradition, and discipline is too strongly anchored in his brain, which has hardly room for any others, for him to miss this occasion, unique in the year and universally awaited, to show this unofficial public how he is getting on and how he is still able to march, even if it means going against the orders of his personal physician, Dr. Lauer.

The public of the Opera Ball is a rather strange mixture. On one hand, the aristocracy and the army come quite freely, since the court is there; the aristocracy occupying the boxes and the dress circle and watching the public circulate without mixing with it and leaving a little after the court leaves—and the army, keeping apart, as it always does. On the other hand, the civilian public that moves about and dances is very mixed: one encounters actors from little theatres and a number of civil servants. It so happens that one whole segment of good Berlin society, not drawn from the nobility nor the army but made up mainly of wealthy intellectuals, feels it is vulgar to set foot at the Opéra Ball. One must hasten to add though that, however mixed this public may be, its behavior is always impeccable. Every German is in fact born dignified, and, as soon as he dons a dress coat, he makes not a single gesture that does not spring from an attentive study of the conduct of his superiors.

As on every similar occasion in this good Berlin in which one lives in a little state of siege, the area around the Opera, on that evening, has been cleared with great care by the mounted police, and, as always, one finds on the edge of the sidewalk this row of poor people, with wan complexions, tow-colored hair, watching open-mouthed and never dreaming of jeering nor uttering the slightest word of protest.

One cannot imagine an opera less lively than the one in Berlin. On the outside, it is a little Greek temple blackened by time, with a wretched entrance, through the bare and filthy wooden door of which no more than two people can pass at a time. On the inside, a hall seating eighteen hundred people; no painted ceilings, statues, nor decorations but just a surface riddled with ugly gilt mouldings; around the hall, a narrow wood-paneled corridor with cloakrooms and two alcoves, one for the woman selling librettos at 25 centimes a piece, the other for the man selling Seltzer water, two little businesses that do quite well. For the past three years, there has been a foyer or at least a concert room that serves as one. A hall completely bare, with a circular divan in the center, it is given over as a foyer to the public, when there is no concert.

At nine o'clock the court arrives. From eight o'clock on, the boxes and the dress circle have been occupied, and it is impossible to move about in the hall. The floor has been cleared of its seats and raised to the height of the stage, which in its entirety is also open to the public. In the mob that moves about, one notices at first naturally nothing but uniforms; dress coats, however, form a good fourth of it. The uniforms are, as always, immaculate. But those dress coats! Here, as in every Berlin salon that has no cosmopolitan pretentions, a well-cut dress coat is a rarity that creates a sensation.

Whoever wears patent-leather pumps instead of the everyday shoe or the short boot so dear to the German virtually has their sheen triumphantly reflected on his face. As for the opera hat, it is often replaced by the silk top hat that has been brushed against the grain by the crowds of twenty balls and is so old-fashioned that one of our country coachmen wouldn't be seen in it. On the other hand, the white ties, which are quite wide, are of satin, and both hands are tightly gloved. Most of these dress coats are covered with decorations; campaign ribbons abound; such and such an actor is decked out with a dozen crosses.

There is always, however, some skeptical and non-decorated Berliner to tell you: "Pay no attention to them; whoever wants the Order of the Red Eagle can have it; as for the Iron Cross of 1870, as you see, it is given to everyone."

What can one say about women's clothes? In vain does a Frenchman arrive in Berlin with the resolution of ridding himself of all preconceptions; he is forced by the evidence to admit that the notion of German bad taste, especially with regard to feminine apparel, is not an idle invention. All one need do, moreover, to clear up the matter is converse with a German lady who has been to Paris and who has her clothes made, if not in Paris directly, at least in some Parisian shop on Unter den Linden. Better still, a German woman who is not a Berliner will tell you quite frankly: "What you see here is not German, but Berlin, taste."

What is especially striking in this clothing is its lack of unity, harmony and discretion. The incongruity among the different pieces often becomes grotesque. Moreover, the Germans have found an inspired signboard for their clothing stores. All these shops, even the most distinguished ones, including the one from which the Empress sometimes orders her dresses, all display rather cynically, this characteristic sign: *Mode-Bazaar*. And indeed all these ladies deck themselves out to suit their fancy with bits and pieces picked up in some fashion bazaar. And then no one has an elegant hairdo or proper shoes. Their walk is awkward, their gestures are unrefined, their voices strong and monotonous, their laughter without nuance.[1]

The boxes and the dress circle naturally present a less incongruous and more correct appearance. They are occupied by that society characterized in Berlin by the extremely German word, *hoffähig*, that is, fitting for the court, worthy of being invited to court.

[1] Laforgue would have been interested to see that German bad taste in women's clothes has found its match in present-day Washington. In *The Washingtonian*, August 1986, prominent Washington women are described as "twinkling feebly in nightmare get-ups of droopy lace, ditzy prints, floppy taffeta, bulging midriffs, dangling purses, cheesy-looking muumuus and snappy strappy shoes."

In the two right stage boxes, some ambassadors' wives. Mme de Courcel never fails to sit in the front row. Ambassadors in informal dress and attachés and their wives fill the two adjoining boxes.

When the Emperor and the court enter, the diplomatic corps and the public rise from their seats and wait until the Sovereign has taken his place. The Royal Family occupy two stageboxes. The Empress, who has but a moderate taste for popularity and for the Berlin public, never appears at the Opera Ball. But last year she took a notion to do so, although she had fainted from weakness that very morning. She was placed in a corner of a stage-box, where she sat motionless and nobly embellished. Berliners who had not seen her for some years, and who will always be unaffected by a certain type of beauty and grandeur, came and went before their forgotten Sovereign, as if somewhat disturbed by this apparition, scarcely daring to approach and gaze upon it.

The public is accustomed to the faces of the Crown Princess, the Princesses Victoria and Charlotte and Princess William. It moves before the royal boxes and can admire them close-up. The Opera Ball is one of the very rare occasions on which the Princesses wear their tiaras and their diamonds. After half an hour of this review, the manager of the royal theatres gives a signal. Then a chorus, seated in a gallery above the stage, sings what is called the *Polonaise*. Preceded by this same manager, before whom the public arranges itself in two tight rows, the court comes down and opens the ball by slowly walking twice in procession around the hall.

This is the ball's most interesting moment and its justification. It is assuredly also, now that he no longer parades on horseback, the moment of the year when, seen from close-up by this chosen public, the Sovereign makes his greatest effort to stand erect once more, not drag his feet when he walks, and to brighten up his eyes and smile. As always, he gives his arm to the Crown Princess, but one can see that it is rather the arm of the Crown Princess that strongly supports his.

The court takes its place again; the dancing begins, but still without much spirit; the army takes the lead; the dress coats wait.

Meanwhile the Emperor, accompanied by an aide-de-camp, leaves his box, circles by way of

the corridors, submits en route to some intro-
ductions, most often of a male or female singer,
newly recruited by the Opera, and then goes
into the diplomatic box to sit down between two
ambassadors' wives, and chat for some twenty
minutes. Chat, alas. The public that sees the
Sovereign move his lips, smile, laugh, curl his
moustaches, and sees these ladies also smile in a
delighted way, that public is deceived. The entire conversation is limited to the Emperor's
vague French monologue. It is useless to answer
him, the fatigue of his mind being at least as serious as his hearing.

One hour later, the Emperor and the court
return to the Palace. With the court's departure,
the boxes and the dress circle are half-emptied
little by little, and little by little also, the diplomatic corps vanishes save for some young attachés who come down to mix with the dancing
crowd, to display their Paris or London clothes
and the impertinence of their French accent.
And in fact, the good Berliner who comes in
contact with them, admires and envies them and
feels that he will never be anything but a Berliner.

As soon as the court has opened the ball, a
quarter of the public, the part that proposes to

dance solidly until dawn, as they do in Berlin and Vienna, has dashed toward the foyer where a buffet and tables have been set up. All the tables are immediately taken. One does not exactly have supper; there's hardly anything to order except oysters, lobster, beefsteak and champagne, which is typical of Berlin.

There is nothing more amusing than to move about among these tables, to lose one's sense of taste in this orgy of grotesque clothing, and to listen to gossip about the Emperor and his court and allow oneself again a little glimpse of German table manners.

At the back of the hall, behind the stage, is set up the inevitable beer-stand. The bare shoulders, the uniforms, the dress coats line up: the bar is never empty. Some enter smiling aggressively as if to say, "What about slumming for a change?" but seem, on leaving, rather unhappy not to have dared go back for a refill. This affectation of at times scorning beer, as not being genteel, is not uncommon. Germans will never completely rid themselves of their French prejudices.

When it no longer senses above it the disturbing presence of the court, nor the probably impertinent curiosity of the diplomatic corps, the public that has come to dance at last feels itself at home and dances as if it were.

Lieutenants' uniforms and dresses accompanied by dress coats mingle little by little. All this society is lively, unfettered by brilliance or bright chit-chat. All cheeks are pink; all eyes shine, even through glasses. Soon the aroma of this ball, a mixture of eau de Cologne and the floor wax that has been very generously applied, is at its strongest. People are no longer ashamed of the beer-stand hidden behind the stage, and the last embassy attaché in his London-made suit with his studded stiff shirt can disappear without anyone's paying the least attention.

Tomorrow's newspapers will report at length on this event, dragging out their elegant enameled French clichés with provincial insistence.

Tomorrow too, all Germany will know that the Emperor has again opened the Opera Ball, that he looked well and chatted with the greatest vivacity. For all Germany, this is the presage of an assured prolongation of life for yet another year. The Emperor has opened the Opera Ball: he will then be present at the great spring parade, will hold his summer interviews, and watch the autumn maneuvers.

8

THE LOVE OF RANK;
TITLES AND DECORATIONS

The love of titles is one of the traits of the German character best known in France. We are especially familiar with the *Wohlgeborener* (the well-born) and the *Hochwohlgeborener* (the superlatively well-born), which are made to precede names on envelopes.

Prussian protocol calls for forty-three categories. (A deputy is in the fortieth category, coming after the lower officials of the court.)

One never omits one's title on any occasion and no occasion to invest oneself with it is lost, no matter how insignificant it may be. For example, a little exhibition of curios, to which collectors have lent things. I have only to copy from the catalogue: Such and such an object lent by

Herr Banker So-and-So; such another by Herr Professor So-and-so . . . or by Herr Broker and even by Herr Stockholder.

There is a certain character at the court whose title is: *Geheimer Hofrat und Wirklicher Geheimer Hofrat von . . . Exzellenz* ("the cabinet privy counsellor, actual privy counsellor to . . . Excellency").

When the historian generally known by the simple name of Leopold Ranke[1] was ill, during the month before he died and when the newspapers gave news of his health, one could read: "The Real Privy Counsellor Professor Doctor Ranke spent a troubled night" (*Der Wirkliche Geheime Rat, Professor Doktor von Ranke hatte eine unruhige Nacht*).

The use of titles is so natural that they are current among people who have been living together closely for years. From time to time, German sentimentality makes of a title an affectionate diminutive. I remember how astonished I was to hear a lady greeting a friend by saying, "How are you, *Geheimräthchen?*" The lady addressed is married to one of these eternal privy

[1]Leopold von Ranke (1795–1886) was Professor at the University of Berlin 1825–71. His desire to relate history with supreme objectivity "as it actually happened" (*wie es eigentlich gewesen*) made him the father of the modern objective historical school.

counsellors, and this title is naturally borne by his wife and now her friend comes to add to the title a cute diminutive ending, as if one would say, "How are you, my little Privy Counselloress?"

This love of titles is contagious: hasn't one seen the famous pianist Mme Essipoff, a mad Russian woman, who has played at court, send in her fee and ask in exchange to be given the title "Court Pianist." This title means nothing and brings her nothing. Mme Essipoff received her title.

In a newspaper one reads: "Frau Hofmeister has just been advanced from *Opera Singer to the Court* to *Singer-in-Waiting*." Which changes nothing at all.

One is familiar with the abuse of *Herr Doktor* and *Herr Professor*.

Herr sounds magnificent. *Der Herr* means at the same time *the Lord* and *this gentleman*.

A waiter speaking to another waiter: "Come here, *Herr Colleague*."

A waiter in a café addressing the head waiter in charge of collecting bills uses his title, "Herr Head-waiter."

A maid, leaving another maid on a doorstep, is heard to say, "Good-bye, colleague."

When one has no sort of title but belongs to

the middle class, one belongs to the *Herrschaften* (exact translation: *Their Lordships*).

A house has a servants' staircase; the bottom of the other staircase bears the words: "For the *Herrschaften* only." A waiter in a café asks: "What will you have, my *Herrschaften?*"

Many shops selling livery. Green material the color of mashed peas and coffee-colored gaiters predominate.

One doesn't see here as in France ribbons and rosettes in buttonholes, with exception, of course, of the large white and black ribbon of the last war; it is seen rather often in the street.

But at parties, receptions and court balls how the chests are filled! I open a year-book. The cross the least given is the one *Pour le Mérite*, a star that bears this French inscription. French, did I say? Not entirely: one would have had to say in French, *Au Mérite*. We know that in regard to this cross, Schopenhauer uttered his sally: "*Pour le mérite!* but all crosses ought to be for merit." This order has four degrees, the last degree being designated: *Für Wissenschaft und Künste* ("For the arts and sciences").

The Red Eagle (*Der Rote Adler*) is not only common but numbers also . . . forty degrees.

The Black Eagle (*Der Schwarze Adler*) is

"simple" and "with chain." Then twenty sorts of orders of the Crown (*Kronenorden*); then sixteen of the *House of Hohenzollern*. Four varieties of the Iron Cross, the cross of the last war (what a pretentious medal!). Two orders of *Johanniter* (*Johanniterorden*). A medal of *Military Merit* (*Kriegsverdienstmedaille*), one of *service* (*Dienstmedaille*), and two *Hohenzollern* medals.

These are but the Prussian decorations. Imagine adding to the constellations on these immense chests: ten from Anhalt, ten from the Grand-Duchy of Baden, fifteen from Bavaria, ten from Hanover, a half-dozen from Hesse (from the Prince) and a dozen from the Grand-Duke, six from Lippe, a dozen from Mecklenburg, ten from Nassau and as many from Oldenburg; twelve from royal Saxony, eight from grand ducal Saxony and six from ducal Saxony, two from Waldeck, eight from Würtemberg; Hamburg, Lübeck, Bremen all have theirs.

These decorations may no longer all be used and some may be completely dead (at least in certain of their degrees) but, in any case, they give you an idea of what this country has produced.

9

UNTER DEN LINDEN

This is Berlin's main avenue, the center of lounging and activity, where everybody goes strolling on Sunday. Everything is there: the Palaces, the University, the Opera House, the Royal Guard House, the Royal Academy of Art, the Arsenal, the Singing Academy, which is the chief concert hall, the Residence of the Commandant of Berlin, the largest restaurants, the brightest shopwindows, the Library, the Aquarium, as well as the only café in Berlin (a magnificent one where you can find newspapers and reviews from the world over).[1] At one end of the avenue, the Museums and the Town Hall

[1] The Café Bauer at the corner of Friedrichstrasse and Unter den Linden, where Laforgue spent many hours.

(*Rathaus*) with its pink tower, and a little farther on, the Stock Exchange; at the other, the
Pariser-Platz with the French Embassy facing
the Officers' Club, and the Brandenburg Gate,
a little triumphal arch that leads to the nearby
Tiergarten. All this can be found lined up in a
space that can easily be covered in twenty minutes. Unter den Linden is, in fact, nothing but a
double row of monuments interrupted in the
center by some twenty shops. And all these monuments look like one another, with broad flat
roofs, from which statues project into the sky;
gray, bare, and cold, they encircle the statue of
Frederick the Great like so many barracks.

Only the half of the avenue running from the
Palace to the Pariser-Platz is planted with trees.
The boulevard is fifty meters wide; down the
center runs a hard clay walk where in summer
babies with their nurses take the air while people
idle about roasting on the benches or quenching
their thirst at the drink stands. This walk is bordered by two rows of linden trees, the last of the
old trees that have given the street its name. The
two narrow outer paths, one a paved, and the
other, a bridle path, were also at one time lined
with trees; but several years ago these trees
suddenly withered and died. Some said it was

caused by leaks in the gas main, while others, more informed as to Berlin ways, blamed the unceremoniousness of evening strollers. Whatever the reason, they have now been replaced by young trees, shored up by thin poles, their roots surrounded by cement.

Why does one say in French "Avenue des Tilleuls?" There is no corresponding expression in German; street signs read and Germans say: "Unter den Linden"—"Under the Lindens." It is quite poetic really and the sentence: "Every Sunday Berliners, on leaving church, go strolling under the lindens," must sound well—from afar.

Life under the lindens is divided in two parts by the troops that pass at noon, a band in the lead, for the changing of the Guard.

In the morning you find every degree of poverty, while in the afternoon there is an air of luxury and leisure.

8:00 A.M. Workmen dragging past, shopgirls with their cheap little hats, four enormous tumbrels chock-full of those red cabbages so dear to the people of the city. In big letters on the side of a lorry stacked with coffins: Coffin Factory, 32 Flower Street. How wretched are the little buses with seats for ten people on the roof.

Two masons drawing a cart loaded with mortar. To another cart a man is hitched by a strap while a woman pushes. Then a number of little carts drawn by dogs, a team of fine muzzled dogs that will soon be on their haunches waiting patiently on a rag while their master stops to have a drink. Wagons are built low because the city is so flat; one never sees a team of horses, and there is little use of the whip. Unlike Paris, Berlin seems a heaven for horses. But, alas, what horses! Sad, skinny, bearded, shaggy-hoofed old nags, with the exception of those that draw the first-class cabs.

Manufacturers or shops do not have special horse-drawn carriages as they do in Paris. This luxury has yet to develop, which accounts for the great number of hand carts and elegant wheelbarrows decorated with medals obtained in exhibitions.

On horseback, two by two, come six grooms of the royal stables, wearing top hats, doeskin breeches, riding boots, black riding coats with buttoned-back red flaps. They are followed back from the Tiergarten by an equerry whose uniform and headpiece look like those of a French general. Also returning from the park is an old brake with four horses and two postillions.

Gradually quite a different sort of activity begins as the workers start to arrive. The Palaces open their gates to their officers and functionaries: there is a coming and going, the military is much in evidence. Here are brokers going to the Stock Exchange in their carriages or cabs. Messengers, wearing red caps marked "Express," are posted on the busy corners. Students stroll in the garden in front of the University, enjoying a brief recess. A hearse with a low chassis comes by with its coachman in a three-cornered Louis XV hat with silver trimming; and already the old woman sits with her knitting in front of the Opera, hawking programs and librettos for the evening performance.

There goes Count Perponcher with his waxed moustaches and his stiff formal civilian dress. The Lord Chamberlain has just had his little audience with the Emperor, as he has every morning. He bows to one of the young ladies-in-waiting ad interim, one who until just a month ago was still ensconced in her provincial castle, and is quite intimidated by being followed at fifteen paces under the lindens by a liveried groom heavy with gold braid.

Finally the Guard. The Emperor reviews it

from his window. Gaping Berlin bystanders and foreigners perched on their carriages lift their hats.

Then the great vacuum of the dinner hour: a few people on one sidewalk, not even a stray cat on the other.

The avenue comes to life as an open barouche passes bearing the Emperor to the Tiergarten at the customary hour. He is slumped over in the same old gray coat with a fur collar; beside him is his aide-de-camp. On the edge of the walk, men lift their caps and bow, women line up and curtsey.

And then the afternoon, given over to strollers, especially officers, bourgeois on their vacations, and bored embassy attachés.

The Emperor returns from the Tiergarten, and soon you may expect to see Herr von Bismarck's closed carriage draw up at the Palace.

At the end of the avenue, solitary and still in his coat, with his yellow mummified face, Field Marshal von Moltke is out for a little stroll. The street doesn't seem to exist for him. He is the *Schlachtendenker*, the "battle thinker." One is reminded that von Moltke is Danish; there is nothing of the German about him. Who can say what he is really like? One thing is certain, and that is that he is less affected than Bismarck. He may be seen in the streets and at all court festivities.

A squad of soldiers, shouldering their rifles, march by to relieve a Guard post; they are led by a squad leader who carries his rifle under his arm. An officer passes. The squad leader shouts a word, and the soldiers present arms and mark time until the officer has passed. The same scene is repeated automatically all day long everywhere in Berlin.

A wagon loaded with little girls off to some party in the country; as they approach the Palace, they break into the national anthem written to the tune of "God Save the Queen."

Two guards stand at attention at the Palace gate ready to present arms to any officer who comes by. At the base of the ramp, three or four policemen. At night two policemen in civilian clothes walk their beat between the two Palaces.

No outfitted carriages anywhere, and scarcely a correct brougham. Peculiar private carriages. A brougham flat as a sedan chair drawn by two horses. And the eternal family landau, and the second-class cabs! When I noticed the increase in first-class cabs, I was afraid that the marvelous second-class cab might disappear: nothing of the sort; they built new ones. And so for a long time yet one will be able to feast one's eyes on these lopsided, jolting, closed vehicles with orange and purple bodies and green wheels, or green bodies and yellow wheels, and other such combinations of colors; with enormous black numbers in white squares on the sides. Inside hangs a large cardboard listing the prices. And the coachman has to be seen to be believed— with his cossack cap, his hip boots, his leather pouch hanging down in front, his filthy beard and his total ignorance of tips.

No equipages, no liveries. Coachmen wear all cuts of beard except the two considered proper by both Frenchmen and the German court, a sergeant's moustache or a full beard. More pitiful than anything else are the hats they wear, which are like the top hats of wandering minstrels. I have seen a private carriage at the Stock Exchange. The coachman was wearing his master's old top hat; the hat was partly crushed, but to it had been attached a brandnew patent leather cockade that caught the sunlight like a black diamond.

The old historian Mommsen[2] steps out of the University holding a pile of books tight against his chest; he slowly crosses the walk and enters the Library.

A nun, the essence of simplicity, with a little light brown hood and a long gray shawl.

Nurses out with children. Babies are never seen in the streets; the pram is unheard-of. Most of these nurses, who come from the valley of the Spree, are perfectly hideous. They wear gaudy bonnets and dresses—usually a wide red ballet skirt with their calves and red arms showing.

A wonderfully groomed foot soldier carrying a valise on which is displayed in copper an enormous count's crown.

A splendid funeral: first the undertaker's mute, then the hearse. The hearse is a square catafalque on very low wheels; topped with a cross on four draped columns. The two horses wear black plumes and their black cloth drags the ground. The coffin, banked with flowers,

[2]Theodor Mommsen (1817–1903), Professor at the University of Berlin and author of the classic *History of Rome*, received the 1902 Nobel Prize for Literature. In his last will and testament he wrote: "I have always been a political animal and have wanted to be a citizen. But this is not possible in our nation in which the individual, even the best one, can never entirely transcend military subordination and political fetishism." See *Imperial Berlin*, pp. 195–96.

rests on a bed of folded crêpe, and displays its horrible yellow varnished wood for all to see. The hearse is escorted by four undertakers. Berlin undertakers are dressed like beadles, in old opera hats and long black coats. Nobody behind the coffin, nothing but ordinary carriages. There are never any special carriages for funerals. No one in the street pays any attention.

Two unemployed workmen drift along in front of the shops. From time to time, they pull out a flask of brandy and take a swig.

A large metal sign has been hung up on the street light in front of the Opera bearing the huge letters black on white: "Open at 7:00 P.M." The poor old woman is still there hawking her librettos.

Boys and girls are coming back from school. They carry rough cowhide bags over their backs like foot soldiers. The little sponges they use for erasing their slates and blackboards hang from their bags. They stop in front of the Arsenal to swing on the chains stretched between the pillars.

There are no newsstands. For a newspaper one has to go to the center of Berlin, to the corner of Unter den Linden and Friedrichstrasse, where a poor old woman stands behind a lattice trellis, displaying German and Viennese papers, the *Times*, the *Figaro*, the *Journal amusant*, the *Petit journal pour rire*. Germans do not read newspapers in the street.

A workman crosses the street carrying in his two hands an enormous jug of foaming beer that washes back and forth like the waves of the sea.

A winter sky; a mounted policeman passes. With their black horses, pendant sabers, and long black coats hanging down on the horse's hindquarters, these policemen are posted at the busiest intersections.

In autumn and in early spring, the sky seems vaster and colder above all these flat-roofed barracks. Seen from afar on certain April evenings, the statue of Frederick creates a nice effect with its little three-cornered hat at an angle, as the sun sets against the triumphal arch, a span of forty telephone wires running just above its head.

At the other end, the Pariser-Platz, one finds a similar group of barracks with flagpoles rising from the flat roofs. The French Embassy is the only building with a bit of balcony and a slate roof. Only in summer when the two fountains are turned on and the swallows dart to and fro does it look a bit more cheerful.

Sunday. The city is small, and one can hear all

the church bells. The Guard gets ready to salute the members of the court as they come back from church, and many choose this hour to shuttle back and forth in their fine clothes between the Palace and the Pariser-Platz. Urchins arrive early and are seated against the iron fence. The sidewalk one takes—for naturally there is, as everywhere, one unfashionable side of Unter den Linden—is so crowded that it is impossible to move except at the pace of this Sunday procession. The officers all wear their campaign ribbons. Those escorting their wives are truly splendid to behold. The number of the military is overwhelming, and hands click in military salutes from one end of the avenue to the other. The Guard will go by at noon, the crowd will disperse, and then gather again. This is the best time to view the clothes and judge the taste of the average citizen.

10

THE STREET

Germans, even Berliners, are not strollers. But as the capital grows and improves and the streets offer more and more distractions, the stroller does, to some extent, exist. But there is no German word, and the chronicler must write: *der Flaneur von Profession*.

The arms of Berlin consist of a bear rampant. Berlin has forty thousand houses and had only half that many twenty years ago. Berlin has a streetcar system, a sky covered with a spider web of telephone wires, electric lighting in general use and, for a year now, small central markets replacing the stinking open markets in the public squares.

There's never any crowding, never a vehicle driven too fast. Horse omnibuses are used only by the working class. But the toy-like low-roofed streetcars, without upper decks, are well thought of; officers in uniform take them every day. The driver stands; instead of our foot bell, he carries in his hand one he rings incessantly. The fare, paid with tickets that are checked, is based on the distance covered; there is no fixed price. Each stop is marked by a pole; no numbers.

The walls are not blackened by obscenities or by "*Viva* this or that."

People do not read in the street; you never see people with leather briefcases under their arms.

No interesting street names: always Augusta Street, William Street, Frederick Street, Charles and Charlotte Street, Dorothy Street, Moltke, Bismarck, Goethe, Schiller Street— no street with any fanciful name except for *Unter den Linden*. No sidewalk cafés.

Street discipline: A delivery boy carrying a pyramid of hat boxes is apprehended by a police sergeant who forces him to leave the sidewalk.

I've never seen any of those little white pastry-vendors. Nor a bootblack. No ambulant craftsmen, no shouts in the street, no hucksters from the markets, no clothing salesmen, no chairmenders, no barrel-vendors, no glaziers. There is, of course, the knife grinder. But this man is sinister: instead of singing to attract his clients, on his grindstone he strikes a hammer that produces a rather unpleasant sound. The benumbed visitor then recalls the Parisian plumber's cheerful whistle.

The postman wears a military uniform with his mailbag attached in front to his belt buckle.

The mailboxes on the streets are completely charming, large wrought-iron affairs, painted blue, pretty to look at. The most extravagant outlays, I believe, have been made for the Prussian post offices. Minister Stephan wanted to make a splash and so little towns with populations of 20,000 inhabitants now have real palaces for post offices.

Messengers stand here and there in red polished caps marked by a number and the word *Express*. For a few cents, they'll take a message for you to the other end of the city. And with what dependability. A dependability one would ordinarily find only in a small city.

Policemen are well protected by their unions: when it rains, presto, the raincoat; in winter, coats with fur collars. On the tips of their helmets are little balls.

Flower vendors (the flowers are inevitably

lilies of the valley) must stand in the street at the edge of the sidewalk. These vendors are tramps, loose women, and gray-haired crones. I am speaking here of the corner of Unter den Linden and Friedrichstrasse.

All dogs are muzzled. Except for mastiffs like the one owned by Bismarck with which well-to-do students strut along, one scarcely sees anything but the poor beasts that drag carts.

Poorly supported public services: almost no watering of the streets; our hoses are unknown. In August, the main streets are intolerable because of the dust; one dies for a drop of water. Snow falls and hardens over, sleds replace cabs and pass with their horses shaking their bells in the silence of the empty streets; you can travel easily like that across the Tiergarten. Then comes the terrible thaw and the ugly galoshes.

What a strange incredible creature is the chimney-sweep. Clad in a tight-fitting black suit like a funereal clown and wearing a top hat, he shuffles along, holding a few tools. With his ghostly movement, he looks like someone who has escaped from a circus. And, with his blackened eyelids, you don't know whether he is looking at you or not.

Berliners are not yet accustomed to their

chimney-sweeps; they still smile at the sight of them. But they are always ready to cheer their firemen. A mad alarm sounds, marking heavy hoofbeats. The way is cleared, and the first fire-carriage passes; in it eight firemen sit facing one another in their great fire hats with lowered flaps; the coachman is flanked by two police-men; and on the runningboard stand two other firemen, one ringing a bell, the other holding a torch daubed with pitch that scatters sparks along his path.

One of the most disagreeable aspects of Berlin is the shortage of water. There's none to be found; the city is completely dry. And the ugly old water pumps that you see here and there! Just pipes with faucets and handles stuck in formless nests of planks.

After eleven P.M. Unter den Linden has been deserted for a long while; carts begin to sweep the dust from Friedrichstrasse, which at this time is the only lively street in Berlin. Lively, did I say? I should say the street where they live it up. What a grotesque and heart-breaking spectacle this fast corner provides! On the steps, five or six old crones hunched over the boxes in their laps groan: "Matches, Matches." Bums stop you with the same offer, calling out, "*Herr*

Baron, Herr Doktor, Herr Professor." And then a man slumped on his crutches selling these same matches. And most astonishing of all is a torso enshrined in a crate on wheels moving about with the help of its hands; it wears a long blond beard and glasses and also sells matches. All these people are hidden away during the day; they are allowed here only after 10:00 P.M. What are allowed at night, and should be also in the daytime, are stands selling oranges. Here they are, the vendors with their carts pulled up, while their good dogs curl up on their rags and sleep with one eye open.

And the demi-mondaine (for Berlin tact has reduced Dumas' word to this level) pounds the pavement incessantly. In the winter it's frightful. Fortunately the lantern of the hot sausage-vendor shines in the distance. The ladies help themselves and eat, leaning over the gutter so as not to soil themselves.

The cafés remain open all night.

Friedrichstrasse opens onto Unter den Linden by the Emperor's Arcade (*Kaisergalerie*), an ultra pretentious and gilded construction. This arcade is the real foyer of this whole area. A Viennese café; then nothing but shops with fake, imitation goods, a whole bazaar of cheap bad taste. And, in the far corner, a shop selling photographs and little booklets like this one: *For men only: night guide to Berlin from 6 P.M. to 6 A.M., indispensable to the foreign visitor, useful to the native; interesting for all; the demi-mondaine of Berlin, etc.*

But far from those lights over there an official slowly makes his rounds, wearing a military cap, carrying a bunch of keys, his saber-bayonet at his side. This is the night watchman. Berlin has no concierges, or rather, those there are do not open doors after 10 P.M. You must always have with you the key to your outside door. If you have forgotten your key, the night watchman, who always has a duplicate, will open your door for a fee of ten centimes.

When told something astonishing, a witty Berliner answers, "I've just watched a night watchman die in full daylight."

The lack of concierges means that the postman must bring the letters up himself and that you must add to your address the number of your floor and indicate if you are to the right or left.

II

POSTER COLUMNS;
BOOKSHOP WINDOWS;
PHOTOGRAPHS OF
CELEBRITIES

Berlin, whose walls and hoardings have never been soiled by advertisements or posters, has a few little columns that are unlit at night, on which are displayed in delirious promiscuity all manner of announcements.[1]

The only ones to reserve space are the Royal Theatres and the Opera. It is worth noting that their official announcements (except for such words as "corps de ballet") are in the Gothic script so dear to Bismarck, while all the other posters are printed in Latin characters.

[1] These cylindrical columns between eight and twelve feet high, known as Litfass Columns, still in use today, were the invention of Ernst Theodor Litfass (1816–74), a Berlin printer.

Here pell-mell is the repertory of one of these columns:

"Death (in large letters) daily reaps his rich harvest! But how many happy days on God's green earth they might have had if they . . ." There follows a remedy for tapeworm.

"Celebration of Sedan, at Schöneberg, in the Linden park. Speech by the Deputy Chaplain of the Court, Pastor Stoecker. Dance—Lights— Military Fireworks."

Celebration in a vast beer garden. *The shelling of Strasbourg, in two parts.* The poster is illustrated by a vulgar tinted lithograph, along with General von Werder's communiqué. That should certainly attract the Alsatians in Berlin.

"A child missing from his family."

"Dog lost, reward offered to the honorable person who finds it."

Two double, quite characteristic, posters: "Tonic for the growth of the beard." "Dancing lessons." Germans are for a long time beardless. All Germans know how to dance and Berliners dance madly.

There is one poster that is a fixture, always green, never larger than one's hand, which some Berliners read every morning; this is the one for 110 d'or, advertising the lowest sort of store on the Pont-Neuf. The interesting thing about this poster is that it presents every day, to rhyme with *110 d'or*, a bit of occasional verse. Generals Thibaudin and Boulanger have each been the butt of their lines.

White is a color that belongs to all and is not, as with us, the property of the state.

The rare illustrated posters are for beer: a goat rampant holding a foaming beer mug: sometimes the mug is held by two students. There is a monk (München, Munich) holding a pewter-covered earthenware pitcher, near a barrel in a frame of hops. The only sandwichman that I have seen for several years in Berlin was also advertising a brewery.

To conclude:

"Meeting of a progressive circle of Potsdam, in such and such a room, a program of speeches."

"Fifty men needed to work on ice-boxes . . ."

Finally ads for restaurants, breweries, pawnshops, and lotteries. Although, as I have said, walls are free of advertisements and sandwichmen unknown, German newspapers are filled with advertisements; the *Vossische Zeitung*, for example, has five or six page supplements.

Bookshop windows. There are very few

bookstores in Berlin. In the entire city, I know of only one quite pathetic open-air bookstall. No national or local displays. None of our series of multicolored volumes, none of our stacks of editions. The booksellers with no speciality (law, medicine) give over half of their windows to French books, the other half to German books mixed with some Tauchnitz editions, Italian and Russian volumes. German novels scarcely have any reprints, except every five years some great success such as that of *Frau Buchholz*[2] three years ago.

The volumes stacked in the stores are by Daudet, Zola, and Ohnet. In Berlin, in the first year of its appearance, 9,000 copies of *Nana* were sold.

A glance at the window of the day. *Glory in Paris* by Albert Wolff, marked *Sensationelle Novität* (Sensational Novelty)—*Baccara* by Hector Malot, marked *Neu! Neu!* (New, new). —Two little volumes supposedly translated from Zola, with covers decorated with a drawing by Mars from the *Journal amusant*. The titles: *Moral Stories* and *Realistic Stories*. Does M. Zola know about this?

Imitations of the miniature books that were

2 *Frau Buchholz*, a novel by Julius Stinde, 1884.

everywhere in Paris three or four years ago, covered with colored vignettes lacking either boldness or wit; with titles such as *Mad Tales* and *Forbidden Tales*. A translation of the *Memoirs of Cora Pearl*. Then German booklets such as *The Future of the French*; *Before the Battle*; *The Menacing Voices of East and West* by a German Cassandra, etc. . . .

When you see a crowd of people gathered around a bookshop window, you can be sure to see displayed either the *Figaro illustré* or the *Revue illustrée* or the *Paris illustré*.

Photographs of celebrities.—First everyone connected with the court, from the Emperor down to Prince Reuss XXVII. I won't linger over them. No man of letters; Geibel[3] during the week he was dying. Not a single painter. But the stars of the Opera and the other theatres, and especially the musicians, virtuosos and composers, the whole musical world. The old classical actor Hase with his row of decorations; the truly inspired young Shakespearian actor Kainz; the old comic actress Blumauer with her six decorations, Mesdames Meyer and Barkany. For the

[3]Franz Emanuel August von Geibel (1815–84), poet and dramatist. His *Gedichte* ("Poems"), which appeared in 1840, ran to 100 editions in his lifetime and earned him a pension from the King of Prussia.

Opera there is Niemann as Sigmund; Frau
Hofmeister as Sieglinde; Frau Vogenhuber in
Die Walküre; Lola Beeth, who has, I believe,
just been engaged to sing in Paris (a pupil of
Mme Viardot, with French training) and the
dancer dell'Era.[4] And then the musicians! The
violinists, Joachim, Ysaÿe, Sarasate, Wilhelmi,
Theresina Tua; the pianists, D'Albert, Rubinstein, the eternal Liszt, Mme Essipoff, Mme
Schumann, who is deaf, Count Zichy, who plays
only with his left hand, for which he has devel-
oped a special repertory (he lost his right arm),
von Bülow, and others. Innumerable pianists.
There are, of course, hundreds of pictures of
Wagner, Brahms, Saint-Saëns. On the other
side of the window some pastors, Stoecker,
Frommel, Cassel and Thomas, and the famous
professors, the surgeon Langenbeck, the histo-
rians Mommsen, Curtius and Ranke, Helmholtz, Dubois-Raymond, and Virchow.

At the center of all, the omnipresent, good
wrinkled face of the Emperor, with his twisted
moustache, always shown in half-length with his

[4]Laforgue was especially attracted by Antonietta dell'Era, a
Sicilian from Messina, who was the leading dancer at the
Opera. In his Agenda for 1883 he tells of buying her pho-
tograph and of going to see her several times. See *Looking for
Laforgue*, pp. 120–21.

decorations, packed as tightly as possible one against the other on his broad chest. Except for a few Opera and Theatre stars, he knows none of the celebrities who surround him, the celebrities of his Bismarckian reign, and has little interest in any of them.

I forgot to mention Bismarck and Moltke because they are everywhere. Both have themselves photographed with one hand tucked in an open tunic, in Napoleon's legendary pose, especially Moltke, the "battle thinker."

12

SHOP WINDOWS

The German is not exactly rolling in money, but the care of his clothes is for him a sacred business. Thus he has often had to be satisfied with appearances. In his book on the French, Karl Hildebrandt, speaking of the Frenchwoman's love of fine lingerie, recalls the good German baronesses who have no decent undergarments under their velvet dresses.[1]

Cheap and smart display, that is the impression one has strolling along before the shops on

[1] Ethel Howard, the English governess of William II's sons, wrote in her memoir: "When this criticism of my clothes went on, all the ladies joining in, I longed to retaliate by telling them that their lingerie showed little proof of taste. What was the good of having all these beautiful top dresses if one was not daintily attired throughout? Anything more plain and ugly than the German ladies' under garments I could not imagine." *Potsdam Princes*, p. 183.

Leipzigstrasse, Friedrichstrasse and in the arcade (*Kaisergalerie*) connecting the latter with Unter den Linden.

There is in particular one type of shop, a real depository of all that is imitation and fake, flourishing here on the main streets and in this arcade. Shops of *Schmucksachen*, costume jewelry, as the sign says. Pearl necklaces for 50 centimes, bracelets at 1 to 4 francs, jewelry of Bohemian and Tyrolean garnet and Berlin iron, metal neckties on fake shirt fronts, fans for three francs and rings! rings! And charms with inscriptions "God be with you. God protect you." And ivory, especially that horrible brooch made of two angels' heads from the painting whose reproduction you find everywhere, the "Madonna of Saint Sixtus" of Raphael in the Dresden museum. An article that all these shops have in great supply is one characteristic of the much talked-of family life: the photograph album to be placed on the parlor table. The number of these shops is extraordinary. They traffic in what is manufactured here and exported with success, what the Hamburg merchants call *good for niggers*.

One interesting observation in passing. The sign on these shops is always *Galanteriewaren* ("objects of elegance"). This expression is an old

French borrowing. Saint-Simon says (Régnier edition, p. 74): "A basket filled with all the objects of elegance given on such occasions."

All that is fake, false, and artificial is so pervasive that most of the other stores accompany the display of their wares with: *Echt! Echt! Echt! Real! Real! Real!*

Let us pass in review, at random, those windows of interest to a Parisian.

The signs are very rarely in gilt lettering; they are almost always black on white, which is rather somber. No picturesque signs such as "Au Bon Marché," "Au Printemps," nor in the country any such as "Au Cheval Blanc," nothing but the name of the owner and the article he wants to sell you.

What whimsical person was it who, five years ago, had a little shop on Leipzigstrasse that lasted a year, I believe, with this sign in French in gilt letting: "*Au Bonheur des Dames*"?

In Paris a shop window is not only a display but something for the pleasure of the eye, whose appearance is changed and refreshed each morning. The windows, which are breast-high, are not crowded, because one isn't trying to show off as much as possible. Here you usually lean over a railing, for the sidewalks are filled with holes and the basement windows slope downward, inviting you to lower your eyes: they are ugly and packed with dusty merchandise. On Sundays the streets change their look in a different way than in Paris with the closing of the shops. Instead of metal shutters, here shopkeepers stretch from top to bottom a piece of white canvas on which their name and business are printed in black.

The shop that immediately dazzles the Parisian visitor is the tobacconist's. This business is unrestricted, of course, and there is consequently great rivalry in the displays as well as in the bargains offered. (I shall speak of them in detail in my chapter on Tobacco.)

Dress shops are called *Mode-Bazaars*. (I have already spoken of the jumbled, strange impression given by that sign.)

Tailors display in French the sign "Haute nouveauté."

Toy shops.—Little doll's houses with Negroes in Prussian uniforms commanded by Prussian sergeants; these are called "African Trading Posts." Barracks, hussars' caps with sabers and sabretaches for children. Many bright-green herbariums (you can't go out here without seeing a child with his herbarium on his back). Then the wooden Algerian rifleman that you find everywhere, with the Prussian-colored target on his chest. For little girls there is always a miniature kitchen with all the drawers and all the labels: pepper, nutmeg, bay leaves.

I have said that there are no shops with imaginative signs such as "Au Printemps"; there are no allusive boards either except for two: a pharmacist, *Apotheke*, is always designated as "At the Sign of the Golden Eagle, the Golden Elephant, the Angel, or the Pelican"; these symbols are always displayed before the sign itself, embossed on a bracket. Some grocery stores also hang over their doors a wooden sugar loaf, as they do in France.

Several small temporary shops, constantly changing place, for the sale of lottery tickets. In their windows there is always a golden Germania or a silver Hercules. There are frequent lotteries with modest prizes.

Many stores selling modern knick-knacks. Polished copper, horrible polished copper, and wrought iron are particularly in demand. Beer glasses, of all styles, smoking sets, services for Moselle wine (Moselle is drunk only in special glasses called *Römer*). A number of bronze reproductions of the Victory column (1871) and of the bas-reliefs that decorate its base.[2]

Delikatessen-Handlung, "dealer in delicacies." That's a charming sign. Here the pork butcher's produce is called *Delikatessen*. This window is pleasing to see, but like the others here, it doesn't hold a candle to similar ones in Paris. In the midst of all these delicacies, there is a bronze pig and a silver one, both under glass bells.

The window most satisfying to the Parisian is the florist's. The flowers are arranged with an imagination and a freshness equal perhaps to those in Paris. But, alas, there's a constant order to this freshness, and with it, something quite German, banal floral lyres with ribbons bearing votive inscriptions.

Bakeries are disreputable-looking; butcher shops are completely without character; and laundries are not to be found.

But what can be found is the coffin store. In the rich quarter there's one with a window

[2]Princess Catherine Radziwill tells of having received as a Christmas present from the Empress Augusta "an appalling thermometer in green bronze representing the Column of Victory in Berlin, which in itself is a hideous monument." *My Recollections*, p. 77.

displaying metal coffins, catafalques, models draped in crêpe, urns for ashes after cremation. There are those in the poor districts with their coffins stacked in the open air and their touching signs: complete selection of coffins, whole-sale prices; coffins of polished oak from 30 francs; coffins for adults, from 15 francs; for children, from 1 franc, 50.

13

THEATRES

Berlin is a musical Mecca. Here one can be educated in concert music for 75 centimes a night, and the Opera offers quite a number of works each season. It is prepared to present successively, in addition to the classic repertory, *Lohengrin*, *The Flying Dutchman*, *Die Walküre*, *Tannhäuser*, *Siegfried*, *Tristran und Isolde*, *Die Meistersinger von Nürnberg*, and even *Rienzi*.

From time to time the Opera substitutes what is called a *Symphony evening*.

A *première* has nothing unusual about it.

It sometimes happens that a foreign singer is engaged for several performances and this singer then sings in Italian while the other artists sing in German. There is nothing shocking about it. Edwin Booth thus came to play in English, Rossi in Italian, and another artist in Russian.

On entering the Opera House, one reads this notice: "Ladies are asked to leave their hats in the cloakroom." Ladies are seated in the orchestra. There are no ushers. No one selling programs or renting opera glasses. Those in charge of the cloakrooms are called "wardrobers." Two alcoves: in one, a woman selling librettos; in another, a man selling glasses of Seltzer water, of which a great deal is consumed.

For a year now there has been a foyer. It is a huge naked white room, lit by electricity. In one corner, there is a counter with cakes and lemonade. A few seats. Everyone moves round in the same direction, except for the officers who stand, stiff and aloof, in the middle.

14

THE MUSIC HALL

The *Reichshallen* is the only real Berlin music hall. The ground floor is given over to the early comers; it consists of movable tables surrounded by chairs: the entrance fee is 1 franc, children, 50 centimes. Those on the ground floor come an hour early. There are thus tables with ten people. The children play, chase one another, climb on and off their fathers' knees; some women crochet, men smoke their cigars, everyone drinks. Up above, a row of boxes, and behind, a balcony. The hall is splendid and spacious like all the halls in Berlin. At the back, a stage; on the curtain are the coats of arms of all Germany. On the program the details of the performances are circled by seven advertisements: two for pianos, one for beer (twenty-five bottles for 3 francs), one for cigars.

The show is always divided into three parts, the intermissions are long, the orchestra plays as if one had come for it alone, which is rather the case with this audience. The whole thing drags on interminably.

The show is composed of a singer, some gymnasts, some variety acts and ends with a pantomime.

The enthusiasm of the ground floor is always the same no matter who the performers happen to be. They are called back three or four times; they are asked for encores until they have none left. And, something very unlike the French, when the audience persists in calling back the artists and continues to applaud, if some *sh*s are heard the *bravo*s cease at once, once more the result of the automatic habit of discipline.

Upstairs as well as down there is a buffet: beer, herring, salmon, hard-boiled eggs, anchovies, caviar, cold veal, tongue, ham, Swiss cheese. One may also have sausages and roast beef with mayonnaise. One may even have hot meat dishes carried to one's table. During the silence occasioned by the agonizing feats of strength, the dominant noise is the clatter of plates and glasses. The occupants of the boxes are too stylish to eat; but the gentlemen and the ladies hold out their beer, clink their glasses, empty them and set them down on the little shelf.

The beer goes quickly; in the corners one sees little barrels that have not yet been carted off.

The "artists" appearing on the program have been seen in Paris and everywhere else. The only native number is that of the singer. Her costume is of the greatest vulgarity, a short skirt, high pink and green satin shoes, a low-cut blouse, gloves with endless buttons, with her virtuous tresses down her back. Waddling like a duck, fat arms marking time with her hand on her heart, little twists of her fingers—that's all she has to offer. Never an eccentric step. When the singer is Viennese, there is less pretention, more suppleness, and her numbers are a little noisier. But Berliners have reason to remember those American and Parisian singers who have appeared here.

15

A BALLET AT
THE VICTORIA THEATRE;
NATIONAL THEATRE
(*DAS SCHAUSPIELHAUS*);
POPULAR THEATRE

The Victoria Theatre presents our ballets from the Eden. Something very German: when *Excelsior* was being performed, before each act, an actor came out to deliver some explanation of what was about to happen. You can just imagine how the Parisian audience would react to such a procedure.

At the moment the ballet *Amor* is the rage. The Crown Princess and the Princesses, her daughters, are in their box; many officers in uniform; young attachés from the Embassies.

The spectacle is repulsive, the tights don't fit and they've taken on as supers anyone who came along. Badly pasted painted paper, hasty gilding, glass beads, patched costumes.

The wise director wanted the ballet to have a

grand finale. And so we behold the proclamation of the German Empire at Versailles, with the Empress Louise, the Emperor's mother, rising above it.

The National Theatre (*Schauspielhaus*) is putting on a play by Paul Heyse, *The Right of the Strongest*, which no Parisian writer would dare present to any director, its characters are so poor and so conventional. The appearance of the young leading man astounded me. Absolutely nothing German about him; but completely, in appearance, a young French engineer, his hair neatly trimmed and a well-cut beard.

Popular Theatre (*Volkstheater*). —A summer evening, after a very hot day. Near the outskirts of Berlin, a vast garden with fine trees, sparingly illuminated with gas globes. A week day. Thousands of good people are taking the air, drinking, smoking, watching a cheap spectacle. Family tables predominate. Mothers nursing their babies. At the back, a theatre with a fairly wide stage. A clown with his Berlin repertory, pathetic gymnasts and a pitiful quartet of eccentric Americans. All the spectators are calm: they eat, smoke, take the air; no witty hecklers; no hooligans. Intermission: people stroll in the garden or enter a hall on the side to dance.

The dancing goes on without the slightest

rowdiness; young girls dance together, a mother whirls her baby about. The curtain goes up again: a great melodrama (they're the same everywhere), handkerchiefs come out of the pockets; then a pantomime with a ballet.

This is the Berlin "Prater"; admission 30 centimes.

On the way back on the same outer boulevard, one catches sight of the *Schultheiss*, a vast beer garden packed with families absolutely quiet.

16

BEER AND TOBACCO

Munich used to be the great city for drinking, but now Berlin is beginning to rival it.

I have spoken of the city's monarchic and military aspect; beer and all that goes with it provides the very air it breathes, if I may be permitted such a metaphor.

Beer halls are everywhere on the increase, and with them goes the *Kneipenleben*, the beer-hall life, a rude breech in the notorious German family life (a woman is never seen in a beer hall).

"The German is ridden by the demon of thirst," Luther said. No other explanation has been found for all this beer.

The beer hall has nothing in common with the café; only beer is drunk there and only certain dishes are served, from sauerkraut and sausage to steak tartare.

The new beer halls in the center of town are models of luxury, comfort and coolness. There's one that has been going for two years in Friedrichstrasse. It is one of the sights of Berlin, an architectural oddity; its new turret dominates all the houses around (a municipal ordinance even had to be passed to prevent it from going any higher), and its façade is curiously painted in fresco. The style of these establishments is what is known as German Renaissance; they are panelled in wood from top to bottom, with the wooden rafters often painted; all around the room runs a counter on which are lined up all sorts of beer receptacles, in porcelain, earthenware, metal, and glass from every period.

The panelling bears inscriptions in Gothic script in praise of God. Here is one:

> *If for long life you would pray,*
> *Lift your six mugs every day.*
>
> *Willst du lange bleiben leben,*
> *Musst du täglich sechse heben.*

All these beer halls have electric lights. The counter is often formed from the half of an enormous barrel, the other half forming a dome above it. The tables are wooden and uncovered; on each one invariably there is a basket of little salted rolls with caraway and poppy seeds to stimulate the thirst, and matches enshrined in a heavy metal case. One scarcely ever asks for *light* or *dark*, but rather for Pilsen, Munich, or Nuremberg beer.

After work, especially in the evening, it is difficult to find a place. The fully laid tables are packed; the air is thick with smoke. Men drink, smoke, chat; conversations are interrupted by long digestive silences. There is not a single pipe, long or short (the picturesque legend of the German pipe should come to an end in France), scarcely a cigarette, nothing but cigars.

Beer is *salonfähig* and even *hoffähig*, which means that it is not out of place in a salon or even at court. The latter acceptance is due, they say, to Bismarck. In any case, the buffets at the balls and the court tables never offer it. [1] The Empress despises beer, which means that this drink pos-

[1] But, as Laforgue has pointed out, beer was served at the Opera Ball.

sesses for certain ladies of the Empress's entourage the savor of forbidden fruit.

One beer that will never make its way to the salons is white beer, a horrible liquid in which the most cultivated people delight. White beer is served in enormous white glass beakers like those in laboratories. The beaker is brought more or less full according to the number of drinkers, and the receptacle makes the rounds to every throat.

Concert halls have what are called *tunnels* where, during intermission, people go to drink. The National Gallery has its little tunnel.

From April on radishes, mustard, and horse radish accompany the beer.

In May out come the joyous posters for the *Biergarten*. These are the Eldorados of summer. A beer hall and, adjoining it, a garden filled with tables and white painted chairs. Some of these gardens, near the suburbs, are immense; at night, in summer, with their gas globes lighting up the trees, and hundreds of full tables drinking peacefully away, they make a Homeric impression.

On one of the first April evenings, when it's still shivering cold, I pass by a beer garden. It is deserted except for two lovers seated at a narrow table; between them, an enormous beaker of white beer.

The May posters give one the best idea of the importance of beer to this city. I enter the Academy of Art; in the entrance hall where suppliers put up their advertisements, I find among them one beginning thus: *To all the sons of the Muse and connoisseurs of beer*. Another poster: *To the connoisseurs of beer. Pure Munich beer! Pure Nuremberg beer at . . . conveniently located near all streetcars*. I almost forgot to mention that I have seen in the window of a music store a *Bierwalzer*, a "Beer Waltz."

Beer calls for tobacco. After a few puffs of smoke, a draught of beer.

As soon as one leaves the French or Belgian coach at Cologne and enters a German carriage, one is struck by the fact that the door of every compartment is furnished with an ashtray. So it is on all German railroads: the passenger always has an ashtray to the right or left.

In Berlin one finds the same ashtray in the boxes of the music halls: in the left corner, the ashtray; in the right, the shelf for one's beer glass.

There are two kinds of tobacconists in Berlin. One has a window display of boxes filled with cigars of all varieties, all prices. The price is marked on each box per each thousand cigars. The notice *Direkte Importation* is never missing. You go in and ask for some cigars. What price do you want? You say so many cents. Whereupon if the merchant doesn't know you, you are sure to be robbed and pay twenty centimes for a cigar that a known client can get for ten. The best thing to do is to look, before going in, to see if there aren't on the counter some half-full boxes, with the sales price marked. After having inspected a half dozen shops, you'll always find one that will offer you cigars like this on sale: buy them and you won't be robbed. It would be ridiculous and almost insulting to enter a shop and buy only one cigar, as is done in Paris; they always come in the half-dozen; and are served to you in a specially prepared little paper bag. You don't enter these shops to get a light as you do in Paris: you must always have your own matches with you, and they aren't expensive.

The other kind of shop does not sell cigars, but rather Turkish tobacco and cigarettes exclusively. The store sign is decorated with Turkish and Russian letters and the window with Turkish pipes and fezes framing little stacks of Turkish or Russian tobacco. This tobacco is rarely

purchased: it is difficult to keep fresh, and besides Germans don't roll their cigarettes. One
asks for ready-made cigarettes, which like pipes
are usually smoked only at home.

There is finally the mixed store selling both
Turkish tobacco and cigars and, in addition, besides the tobacco and packages of French cigarettes, a quantity of American pipe tobaccos and
American cigarettes. Bird's eye, Durham, Lone
Jack, Fox tobacco are excellent pipe tobaccos,
but the cigarettes! And one should add the excellent Varinas from the Dutch colonies.

At Christmas, the displays are made more at-
tractive: the boxes are lined up with the cigarettes in gilt paper rings. Cuba! Bahia! Manila!
Havana! Carolina! Christmas presents!

Germans smoke everywhere. In stores they
keep their cigars in their mouths. At the last
beaux-arts exhibition in Berlin, at the entrance
to the picture galleries was a "No smoking"
sign.

You can imagine the host of articles that go
hand in hand with cigar smoking. Everywhere
there are cigar stands of polished copper or
wood. Most Germans have among the trinkets
on their watchchains small instruments for cutting cigar tips.

Shops selling large German pipes with porcelain bowls painted with portraits of the Emperor and Bismarck are everywhere. These pipes are indeed smoked, they are nationally known, and statuettes of Herr von Bismarck seated in his armchair holding this peace pipe are also available. But even in smaller, portable sizes, these pipes are never seen in the street or the beer hall. To see one you must go to some student's room. But I have happened on a concierge taking the air outside his door one summer evening smoking this large pipe. And yet, on the whole, only cigars count, and they are taking over more and more.

17

AT THE RESTAURANT

Dinner at a restaurant is *prix fixe* and *à la carte*; the price of dinner in the finest Berlin restaurant is four francs.

As an average type I'll take a good restaurant where a dinner costs 1 franc 50 (you wouldn't find any in Paris at that price). The place has a regular clientele: the young employees of some ministry who address one another as "Herr Count," "Herr Baron," a half dozen artillery officers always in uniform and middle-class couples; one table is reserved for some members of the Landtag. Luncheon is served there from one o'clock on; a really chic restaurant serves only after two o'clock.

A customer comes in, sits down at your table, greets you and wishes that "your meal be blessed." What generally happens then is that, officer or civilian, he plunges his two hands into the side-pockets of his suit, and draws forth two little brushes, and there he is, with both hands, vigorously arranging the hind part of his hair, bringing the hair on both sides over his ears. (This is the elegant coiffure affected by everyone. Ordinary soldiers have standing orders to have their hair up over their ears.) When that is done, he waits for his soup, and sometimes files his fingernails while waiting.

Of what do bad German table manners consist? First of all, Germans eat with their knives, lifting whole mouthfuls on the blade and carrying them to the mouth, and, on withdrawing the blade, gripping it in the teeth, without ever causing a flow of blood! And this is seen not only at the table of poorly brought up people but everywhere, even at court tables. Some use the knife thus for all dishes. They use the fork only to lift lumps of puree and mustard which the knife smooths over and over. Their style of carving is atrociously vulgar: they do not hold the knife and fork forward and up but carve by extending the elbows. The rest is made up of twenty little horrors that take place "between the

plate and the lips," all concluded by the gross
obsession of hiding the mouth with one hand,
while cleaning the teeth with the other.

I verge dangerously on caricature, but I cannot forget a good German of fine middle-class
stock, a regular customer at this restaurant. I
can see him, huge and blond in his glasses, eating, his nose in his plate like those Bruttium
herdsmen of whom Flaubert speaks, cutting off
every mouthful of bread with his knife, taking
his bottle by the bulge (and with what five fingers!), lifting his glass of Moselle and looking
at it in the light, first wetting his lips, then guil-
tily drinking from it and hurling himself afterwards back in his chair and stroking his shapeless beard.

People smoke at all times in restaurants. As
soon as the restaurant opens, you can come and
bolt your lunch, then proceed to smoke up the
room for the sake of those who follow. There is
always on the table at which you sit, beside the
basket of rolls and toothpicks, a matchbox enshrined in its castiron ashtray.

The rolls of which I have just spoken are no
larger than your fist; a single one is all a German
needs to accompany an entire dinner, and he
consumes half of it with his soup, not *in* his

soup, but *with* it. Frenchmen astonish the waiters by constantly ordering rolls, but are not
made to pay extra for them. (The Frenchman,
who in the Middle Ages was called "Jean Far-
ine," has always been known for his love of
bread.)

After five or six o'clock the *prix fixe* menu disappears and is replaced by a menu as large as a
small newspaper, divided into hot dishes and
cold dishes. On this menu, the prices are greatly
augmented but the helpings and the cooking are
quite different. One dines with this menu until
eleven at night. It is pleasant to dine in the evening, by lamplight, for one of the horrors of the
day disappears: the general filth of the waiter's
dress coat.

German cuisine is recognized as the worst
in the world while the French is considered the
best. (Bismarck himself recognized the fact
when he said France was made to give the world
barbers, dancers, and cooks.) Many restaurants
place on their posters or their announcements
the words: "French cuisine." Those whose patri-
otism is offended by this homage put: "Viennese, French, and German cuisine."

A Frenchman is amazed when he hears, and

furious when he finds from experience, that restaurants in Berlin open only at one, two, or three
o'clock in the afternoon. The Grand Hotel in
Berlin even serves full meals only after four
o'clock. For fear of cutting off one's appetite,
one wanders about famished from noon until
one or two. When the sacred hour arrives, one
sits down to a great parade of dishes. And then
leaves. The afternoon has scarcely begun and
one is overcome with sleep, incapable of doing
anything. Many Berliners protest against this
absurdity, but reform is difficult, even in families for it upsets the visiting hours. Would you
believe it that at three o'clock in the afternoon
you cannot enter a museum because the employees are having lunch to be followed by a siesta!
People are counting on the reign of the Crown
Princess to change this pattern: it seems that she
will set an example and impose it on others.

It is needless to add that Germans eat enor-
mously. Every café and every beer hall has cold
things ready to serve. Theatres (except the two
royal theatres), and music halls always have a
buffet: you don't just go there for refreshments,
you may have an assortment of caviar, smoked
tongue, cold lobster with mayonnaise, Swiss
cheese on a roll, salmon, anchovies, hard-boiled

eggs, cold veal, and ham. At the entrance to the National Gallery there is a sign saying that the buffet is to the right. You find this sign again in a room on the second floor, beside "The Forge" by Menzel.

The finest orchestra in Berlin, the Philharmonic, plays before a hall of beer drinkers. On certain days, as visible as possible, there is a sign reading "Today fricassee of partridge."

N.B. As soon as it gets warm, the waiter will recommend to you, instead of a potage, cold soup or "beer soup." Answer, "No, no, never!"

18

SCHOOL OF FINE ARTS;
EXHIBITIONS OF
STUDENTS' WORKS;
ARTISTS

There is no sacrosanct tradition as there is with us: these students work naively at their art and do what they like. They have the same courses we have, plus a workshop for landscape painting and a workshop for drawing and for the painting of animals.

The exhibition of students' works would make our school laugh, students and professors alike. The general impression is of a finishing school exhibition. Very few live models, many drawings done from figures in the round, carefully executed plates of anatomy, pencil drawings of ladies; still-lifes (skulls and beer glasses), entire rooms filled with little bits of pencilled nonsense, all painstakingly signed; and even caricatures, humorous vignettes for the newspapers, titles and letters wreathed and embellished.

There are at least ten professors in the school.

While waiting for the opening of the Salon (the Menzel show), I stand in the entrance hall. Some students are there. They all wear the vast felt hat called a "Rubens" and are tightly gloved. Politely bowing, they give information to the ladies. One of them with his "Rubens" at an angle, is curly-headed and wears a velvet vest and bell-bottom pearl-gray trousers with trouser straps. They all give themselves airs and exaggerated manners; none looks the least bit seedy. I glance at the billboard: advertisements for restaurants and beer halls and several costume rentals for historic parades (these costume parades are the students' passion; they arrange one on the slightest pretext.)

There is an artists' club, a veritable cellar. I spent one evening there: such an evening consists in sitting around a table with one or two people drinking and even eating while listening to the noise of a neighboring billiard table. On the walls around the room are portraits of completely unknown artists. And mottoes: first the philosophic, very German, always empty, one, such as: "Time passes quickly toward eternity." Then the artistic motto: "God created man from clay; try—it is also within your power." A copy of the fake Rubens from the Museum. To this cellar is attached, a few steps above, a lighter room in which are exhibited, when the opportunity presents itself, "sensational paintings" that happen to be passing through Berlin: the "Christ" of Munkácsy, the "Two Sisters" of Giron, the "Jacquerie" of Rochegrosse.

Berlin Salons are irregular; there is no special exhibition hall. For some years, in fact, there has been no Salon at all. Admission is 50 centimes. It would be out of keeping to speak here of German art. With the exception of that extraordinary genius, Adolph Menzel, this art is inferior to that of France, Belgium, Holland, Italy, and Spain.

In an artists' supply window is displayed a booklet on "How to become a connoisseur of painting in sixty minutes"—second printing.

Although musical criticism is interesting and competent even in the smallest daily paper, art criticism is worthless.

There are three galleries exhibiting canvases in their windows. Two of them on Unter den Linden exhibit scarcely anything other than the eternal Italian views of Achenbach, views of Switzerland by some inferior Calames, some sentimental family pieces by Knut-Ekwald, some Egyptian dancing women by Sichel, and the like . . . and this display seems to last forever. For the past year, one of these shops has been taken over by a Cologne merchant who organizes little exhibitions like those in the rue de Sèze, but how pitiful they are. And then admission to these exhibitions is one franc, something unheard of until now.

The third of these stores is located on Behrenstrasse, the first street immediately parallel to Unter den Linden. It is the only artistic shop in Berlin; the proprietor, Herr Gurlitt, a very intelligent young man, is informed on all that is going on in art beyond the German border. The shop is small and cramped, but there are from time to time excellent exhibitions, sometimes of several masters, sometimes of a single one. On one memorable occasion he had the audacity to put on an exhibition of French Impressionists.[1] If Berlin becomes at all artistic, it will be thanks to Herr Gurlitt.

[1] Of this exhibition in October 1883 Laforgue wrote to his friend Gustave Kahn: "Berlin is busy laughing its head off at a little show of Impressionists that for my part I have always adored, ever since I've known them in fact." The exhibition contained paintings by Monet, Pissarro, Renoir, and Boudin; also perhaps Manet's *Le Chemin de fer*, Mary Cassatt's *La Tasse de thé*, and *Courses de gentlemen* of Degas. The exhibition prompted Laforgue to complete his pioneering essay on Impressionism. See *Looking for Laforgue*, pp. 141–42 and *Selected Writings of Jules Laforgue*, pp. 190–97.

19

THE RACE

One can see at once that this is a race not overly refined by luxury.

No civilized pallor; no nervous physiognomies or appearances; complexions are ruddy, hair—and this is the general rule—in crew cuts, brushed straight back from the middle of the forehead.

In a wealthy district I meet young boys and girls leaving school: their voices are gross, without any nuance of intonation.

Women: handsome foreheads, naturally clear eyes and light hair. English, Dutch, Hungarian, Swedish women all have faces of very varied types. But watch, for example, one Sunday a boarding school of little English girls leaving church and you will sense the abyss that exists between a race that has centuries of culture behind it and a poor race that has been comfortably established for only a single generation. Here also the young Jewesses whom you meet every morning with their music cases provide a notable contrast with the ordinary German women; you feel the presence of a figure in their tight-fitting dresses; they carry themselves well; one must add to that their predilection in dress for dark and warm colors.[1]

The size of a woman's foot is not a myth. In the park your attention is drawn by the feet of the horsewomen. But who is there to fit them out properly in Berlin? There is no proper bootmaker. As soon as you move into Belgium or Switzerland, the size of the German foot, standing out in its isolation, is striking. Only the officer takes proper care of his shoes, but his foot is squeezed in and looks like a sausage roll; it is rather like his tight trousers about which he says to his tailor: "If I can get them on, I won't take them."

The ideal German: the type of modern war-

[1] In one of his notebooks Laforgue writes of the beneficial effect of the infusion of Jewish blood on both German industry and German art.

rior in the bas-reliefs of the last war as contrasted with the Latin. No pretention of refinement, not even the fear of being treated like a Goth, a Visigoth, or an Ostrogoth: a wide open face, broad bushy beard, hair brushed straight back in the middle of the head: in short, the popular figure of the present Crown Prince.

An opposite but still very German type: a delicate build, an irregular reddish beard, hair growing low on the forehead, glasses.

In a little watering place on the terrace of a hotel. Young German ladies seated around a champagne bottle wrapped in its napkin. A young *Referendar*, a cigar in his mouth, serves them and makes them laugh. The cheeks, and especially the girls' hands, redden as they shriek. "*Nein! So! Wann denn? Jawohl! Ach Gott!*" A blonde laughs so hard that her pince-nez keeps falling off.

A student used to tell me that the German woman is more naive than the Frenchwoman, more natural, and consequently easier, more sensual, and more spontaneous. She does not possess, like the civilized Frenchwoman, that skepticism that makes for three fourths of feminine virtue.

20

GEMÜT

Although Germans proudly tell you that you have no equivalent for Gemüt in your language, they themselves find it exceedingly difficult to define. Gemüt is the misunderstood German soul, poetry, nature, intimate family life, etc.

In a little watering place, on the edge of a forest, there is a plank nailed to a tree trunk. Can it be a police ordinance, a road sign? No, it is a few lines of verse intended to impress you with your happiness in being here:

Surrounded by the sweet-smelling foliage of
the woods,
How the heart rejoices, how boldly

Man's thoughts arise in his breast!
Through the branches moves a heavenly breath;
Good-bye to care, good-bye as well
To life's little troubles.

Certain family newspapers offer regularly in prominent Gothic script one of these pedantic empty sentences so dear to the German. In a women's newspaper, for instance, the motto for the day is: "Let people speak ill of you, but live so that no one will believe a word of it." This paper is largely written by its subscribers. Among the articles: "How to stop children from tearing holes in their stockings," signed: *A Saxon Mother*; "How to make Humboldt soup, how to clean umbrellas," etc.

The familial nature of the German soul is indicated by a mania for birthdays and jubilees. A coachman, for example, celebrates his twenty-fifth year on the box. The whole thing is carried to the point of caricature when a husband announces a jubilee on the occasion of the tenth good drubbing he has received from his wife.

There is also a passion for *Vereine* (associations): Berlin has eight hundred such associations out of a total population of a million. But this means that men must meet and drink, and so, like the beer hall, causes a further breach in family life.

A man who has been honored writes on the fourth page of a newspaper among the death and marriage notices: "My profound thanks for the large number of greetings, telegrams, and wonderful floral offerings on the occasion of the twenty-fifth anniversary of my wine business . . . etc. . . ."

One is struck by the quantity of photograph albums that are sold to grace the living-room table; as well as articles for parlor magic, and items designed to provide merriment on picnics. The latter all have to do with music: music boxes, singing birds, musical beer mugs, musical cigar holders . . .

Photographs in the windows of professional photographers often show fathers with their children on their shoulders. I have also seen this particular family group: a husband and wife with two places set at their dinner table, and a centerpiece of flowers; the woman is in a house dress with her hair down while the husband, whose hair is curled, has on a light-colored vest and riding boots!

Writing paper stamped with proverbs is sold everywhere. Naturally these proverbs are always solemn, empty German ones. For example: "First reflect, then begin." Or, on the other hand, something to divert the recipient, an inkspot with this witticism: "Ah, fatal blow!" On April Fool's Day one finds at the stationers a whole array of jokes to send out.

In the drawing room of a noble provincial family, I came across a *Know Yourself Album*. Every page of this album contains an oval waiting to be filled with the appropriate photograph of the victim; and on the other side of the page a column of questions to be answered. The heading reads: "Memorandum for the personality traits of girl friends and boy friends." Then an epigraph, a pompous couplet by Schiller, then a signed introduction followed by a poetic greeting to girl friends and boy friends. We are all familiar with this sort of album, at least with its French equivalent. The one I leafed through had a supplement containing two quite German questions: "What is your favorite dish? What is your favorite drink?" The replies to these two questions are usually caviar, Italian salad, and champagne. (Never the slightest mention of beer.) Other questions: "Who is your favorite artist?" Raphael, Hildebrand, Canova, Deffregger, Thorwaldsen . . . And your poet? . . .

Heine, Dante, Geibel . . . Your favorite Christian name? . . . Wanda, Hildegarde . . . Your favorite historical figure? . . . The Great Elector, Frederick the Great, Gustavus Adolphus . . . Your favorite character in poetry? . . . The Don Carlos of Schiller. The historical figure you hate most? Napoleon, Louis XIV . . . One must also give one's temperament; the young lady had carefully written "melancholy." The page ends with your motto; here is a characteristic one (and I am not just making it up): "Try everything, choose the best."

Happy album owner, when melancholy Wanda comes to dine, you'll know she wants Italian salad and Moselle, if not champagne.

Little family jokes can be carried to a point of the most loathsome silliness. German babies are said to come from storks' nests. So at Easter there is a wild display of these things. One finds everywhere on sale naturalistic photographs of the nests with babies saying as they emerge from the eggs:

> *It was so peaceful in my small home.*
> *Here I am out at last.*

Another baby emerging from an egg says: "May I come? Please ask your wife . . ." and an-

other: "Please talk to your husband about it."
And another: "Greetings, world!" Such is the
Easter display; there is also an abundant supply
of ultra-sentimental photographs that never
leave the shop windows and are sold every day of
the year.

People in France make fun of German couples holding hands in public; it is not very frequent, and yet you do see it at times. I have seen
something of the kind that is quite unique: a
couple sitting side by side in a restaurant; after
every course, they would clasp hands until the
following course, and then after each new
course, begin again, all without uttering a
word.

There is no hesitation about parading one's
family feelings. All newspapers print, among
their classified advertisements, notices of deaths,
weddings, and engagements, which are written
in the most intimate style. They all have columns for the lovelorn, of which this is a sample
entry:

> *Widower, with an income, at the finest time
> in a man's life. Protestant, of quiet cheerful
> disposition, owner of a flourishing business in
> which the intervention of a woman would not be
> required, the father of two sweet well-bred*

children, boy of ten and girl of eight, seeks middle-aged unmarried lady or widow as second life companion. She must possess a sweet disposition and be of healthy body; she must have a real feeling for the home and be ready and able to act as a mother to the children. Dowry of 15,000 francs cash demanded. Strictly confidential; photograph not required.

Another type of marital entry:

Medical student, with excellent future, seeks lady of good family, Catholic, who would advance him the money necessary to complete his studies. Would marry if necessary. Completely confidential; word of honor.

Poor student! And yet not so poor; he will surely have found what he was seeking: there is still some romance left in Germany.

Germans speak of the German soul, German feeling, German family. Their literature, however, has little to say on the subject. Russians keep quiet about it, but all we needed was four or five of their novels to see something entirely different from this Germanic soul, feeling, and family.

21

DRESS

As for German women, the question is settled: they don't know how to dress. Why don't they learn?

The male Berliner takes extraordinary care with his clothes, and those clothes are, of course, influenced by military uniforms; everything is tight and stiff.

Boots are worn nation wide. A gentleman comes to call, sits down, his trouser leg works its way up to reveal the top of his boots with their unpolished folds. Boots, lined with green, are the pride of children on Sundays.

Love of the dumpy look with square shoulders, enormous waist and tight-fitting jacket, outlining a huge rear-end, high heels, hair parted behind, stiff collar, trouser straps, gloves hermetically buttoned, a little light-weight hat and a light cane.

Scarcely anyone except tailors and chimney sweeps wears a top hat; men wear either a very small felt hat or a Rubens with a wide brim.

I can't help admiring the perfection of their shoe-polishing. All their shoes seem to have emerged from a bath of black ivory. On the other hand, they go out in the evening wearing ankle-boots that seem systematically unpolished.

The dress coat is common here. It is never seen at the Opera, but everybody has one; it's as good a suit as any. Waiters wear dress coats, even waiters in miserable cheap restaurants. Sad-looking dress coats they are. Just as there is no good bootmaker here, so there is no good tailor. The dozen or so well-dressed gentlemen that Berlin possesses get their clothes in Paris or London. . . .

The opening of the Exposition for the Centenary of Berlin Salons: Dress coats of burnt soot-colored cloth; one man in a black suit with white trousers; dress coats buttoned up with the tips of their white vests showing at the bottom; watch-fobs, shabby opera hats, large satin cravats. Two or three well-dressed painters are pointed out; they prove to be Belgians.

Workmen do not wear dustcoats but frock coats; officers wear frock coats; street sweepers wear frock coats with their rubber hip boots.

At Baden-Baden it is pitiful to see an officer in civilian clothes stroll in the casino among the elegant Englishmen and Russians, with his unmatching coat and trousers, his well-buttoned gloves, his soiled hat, his cheap cane.

All Germans—all—have rings.

It would be too easy to point out the ridiculousness of much of the Sunday attire. Suffice it to say that one may see a gentleman in a velvet jacket, open shoes with trouser-straps which let one see the white line of his socks—or a young boy, his mother's pride and joy, in civilian clothes, with a plumed hussar's cap and a blue sailor's collar.

To sum up, the dress of the German man and the German woman contrast perfectly. The woman is slovenliness itself; the man, on the other hand, laces himself up tightly, emprisons himself in close-fitting clothes, and parades stiffly about.

22

POLITENESS

Germans are born simple. Their passion for formality comes from their having been so widely called barbarians and boors. They call us impolite; we shall be as polite as they, so they think. The only difficulty is that by working so hard they have put their foot in it.

The great vast dips of the hat that people give to one another in the street seem, at first sight, a friendly joke. They are nothing of the sort. Three gentlemen meet three other gentlemen. They stop and chat; when they leave one another all six hats are raised and remain suspended for a moment in mid-air, all describing a similar parabola.

The same thing goes for bowing. Germans

do not nod their heads but rather their spines. There is also the *Knix*, which all little German girls do mechanically. The *Knix* is that curtsey that consists of briskly bending one knee.

I enter a *Konditorei*, one of those pastry shops where one can take refreshment, with a lady of the best breeding, but one completely German. As we leave, a waiter, an ordinary waiter, opens the door; the lady bids him "farewell" with the most elegant smile.

In shops Germans take off their hats but keep their cigars in their mouths.

A German gentleman and then a young girl enter your railway compartment when the train stops at a station. They both say, "Good morning" or "Good afternoon."

A gentleman you do not know sits down at the same table with you in a restaurant and greets you by saying, "*Mahlzeit*" (abbreviation for *gesegnete Mahlzeit*, "May your meal be blessed!"), and on leaving, says "Good-bye."

Between noon and three o'clock, if you happen to be leaving a store or a café, the shopkeeper or the waiter will greet you with *Mahlzeit*.

Heine said: "In Paris, when someone steps on my foot, I know he must be a Prussian." And that is certainly not just a joke. In the streets of Berlin one is bumped, jostled disastrously, even on a narrow sidewalk, and people don't excuse themselves. Moreover, I deliberately strike with the toe of my shoe the heel of the gentleman in front of me; he doesn't even bother to turn around. A woman who is shoved pays no attention whatever.

In a salon or at any gathering Germans dispense with the necessity of having to be introduced; they introduce themselves, greet you and say quite simply, "My name is such and such," and you are expected to reply, "And mine is such and such."

The first time this happens, one mistakes it for a provocation.

23

GERMANY

Before the good war, the German pictured himself in military works of art as revengeful and fierce. If there is a *furia francese*, there is also a *furor teutonicus*. But since the war, the German sees himself as calm and confident: as portrayed by this delightful image in the *Cologne Gazette*, "The man of the *Landwehr* will place his large hand on the Parisian volcano."

This hypocritical attitude shows itself in the bas-reliefs of a frieze decorating the façade of the military academy.[1]

---

[1]The bas-reliefs of the sculptor Johannes Pfuhl (1846–1921) in the Field Marshals' Hall in the Military Academy (Kadetten Anstalt), Berlin-Lichterfelde, which was destroyed in World War II and occupied after the war by the United States Army. The Military Academy had been estab-

Infantrymen, fully equipped, depart, calm and confident, and, as they return, make triumphant gestures. A cuirassier gets on his horse. An infantryman grasps the hand of his fiancée— it must be his fiancée—who holds a basket on her arm. A second cuirassier embraces his wife, a hefty and noble frau, holding her legitimate baby in her arms. Then two young girls who are engaged: one is desolate, depressed; the other stands straight with eyes raised. An old man, eyes lifted heavenward, places his two hands on the head of a bearded warrior who bows, helmet pressed against his thigh. And finally, this group: a handsome peasant lad quaffs a glass of beer with a shock-headed soldier: a waif holds in his hand a pair of military boots that he must give up, looks at them for a last time, and beside him, a young woman, of splendid physique, with a lofty and serene brow, her German tresses hanging down her back, kneels before a little keg of beer, turns the tap and fills a mug.

---

lished by William I in 1873; the Field Marshals' Hall displayed, in addition to portraits of the Prussian kings, the German Emperor, and the Field Marshals of the Prussian Army, the sword of Napoleon I, captured at the battle of Belle-Alliance, near Waterloo. Pfuhl's bas-reliefs, in a frieze at eye-level along one wall, depicted scenes of the Franco-Prussian War.

REFERENCES

Reference is made in the notes and the introduction to the following volumes:

Arkell, David. *Looking for Laforgue: An Informal Biography*. Manchester: Carcanet Press; New York: Persea Books, 1979.

Aronson, Theo. *The Kaisers*. Indianapolis and New York: The Bobbs-Merrill Company, 1971.

Howard, Ethel. *Potsdam Princes*. London: Methuen and Company, 1916.

Laforgue, Jules. *En Allemagne: Berlin, la cour et la ville; Une Vengeance à Berlin; Agenda*. Introduction and notes by G. Jean-Aubry. Paris: Mercure de France, 1930.

Laforgue, Jules. *Selected Writings*. Edited and translated by William Jay Smith. New York: Grove Press, 1956; Westport, Connecticut: Greenwood Press, 1972.

Masur, Gerhard. *Imperial Berlin*. New York:
Basic Books, 1970.

Radziwill, Princess Catherine. *My Recollections*.
New York: James Pott and Company, 1904.

Smith, Alson J. *A View of the Spree*. New York:
The John Day Company, 1962.

Other books consulted:

Fisher, Marc. *After the Wall: Germany, the Germans
and the Burdens of History*. New York: Simon &
Schuster, 1995.

Laforgue, Jules. *Berlin, der Hof und die Stadt*.
Translated from the French with an afterword
by Anneliese Botond. Frankfurt am Main:
Insel Verlag (Insel-Bucherei Nr. 94), 1970,
(second printing) 1981.

Reissner, Alexander. *Berlin 1675–1945: The Rise
and Fall of a Metropolis. A Panoramic View*.
London: Oswald Wolff, 1984.

Topham, Anne. *A Distant Thunder: Intimate
Recollections of the Kaiser's Court*. New York:
New Chapter Press, 1992.

Vizetelly, Henry. *Berlin under the New Empire:
Its Institutions, Inhabitants, Industry, Monuments,
Museums, Social Life, Manners, and Amusements*.
London: Tinsley Bros., 1879; New York:
Greenwood Press, 1968.